Quick & Easy

JAPANESE
SNACKS
&
LIGHT MEALS

PUBLISHER REPRESENTATIVE OFFICE

Prime Communication System
2-6-8, Shimouma, Setagaya-ku, TOKYO, JAPAN 154-0002
Phone: 81-33-487-8187   Fax: 81-33-410-6379
E-mail: Y1223M@aol.com

AUTHOR'S SALES AGENCY: A.K. HARANO COMPANY
P.O. BOX 1022, Edmonds, WA 98020
Phone: (425)774-5490 E-mail: C_books@hotmail.com

OVERSEAS DISTRIBUTORS

UNITED STATES: JP TRADING, INC.
400 Forbes Blvd., Unit 3
South San Francisco, CA 94080
Phone: (650) 871-3940
Fax: (650) 871-3944

MEXICO: Publicaciones Sayrols, S.A. de C.V.

COLOMBIA: Jorge E. Morales & CIA. LTDA.

TAIWAN: Formosan Magazine Press, Ltd.

HONG KONG: Apollo Book Company, Ltd.

THAILAND: Central Department Store Ltd.

SINGAPORE: MPH DISTRIBUTORS (S) PTE, LTD.

MALAYSIA: MPH DISTRIBUTORS SDN, BHD.

PHILIPPINES: National Book Store, Inc.

KOREA: Tongjin Chulpan Muyeok Co., Ltd.

INDONESIA: C.V. TOKO BUKU "MENTENG"

INDIA: Dani Book Land, Mumbai (Bombay) 14

AUSTRALIA: BOOKWISE INTERNATIONAL

GUAM, SAIPAN AND MICRONESIAN ISLANDS: FUJIWARA'S SALES & SERVICE

CANADA: MILESTONE PUBLICATIONS

U.S.A.: MASA T. & ASSOCIATES

U.S.A. (HAWAII): HAKUBUNDO, INC.

First Edition 1991, 5th Printing June 2001

Original Copyright © 1991 by Yukiko Moriyama

ISBN4-915831-01-9

Printed in Hong Kong

FOREWORD

Today there is a new generation of gourmets who have a deep appreciation of fine foods, and who take pride and pleasure in their preparation. Also the informal meal is especially suited for today's life style. This book will guide you through simple techniques for preparing the basic ingredients contained in easy-to- follow recipes. This book's emphasis has been placed upon the preparation of dishes used in Japanese snacks and simple meals.

As you gain proficiency and personal confidence in simple meal cooking, you may like to go on to Japanese cuisine. I have written another cookbook, JAPANESE CUISINE FOR EVERYONE, in which I offer recipes from Japan including the use of *TOFU* (soy bean cake), *MISO* (soy bean paste), and *SUSHI*. You may adapt various recipes to your own personal taste and experiment with different ingredients to achieve the desired result. I encourage you to go beyond the recipes in this book, by substituting ingredients. Most of the contained recipes serve one to two persons. These amounts allow flexibility, and can be doubled successfully. Some of the necessary ingredients, however, may be unfamiliar to you. They are listed on page 97, and are available at most Oriental food markets.

It is my pleasure to share these recipes with you, and most importantly, have fun and enjoy cooking.

May, 1991

Yukiko Moriyama

CONTENTS

CONTENTS

ACKNOWLEDGMENTS

I would like to express my heartfelt gratitude to SHIRO SHIMURA, publisher of JOIE, INC., and his wonderful staff for their trust and faith in my work.

Also I would like to give special thanks to the following individuals for their support, encouragement and patience throughout many months of compiling the materials in this book:

SEICHI ISHIHARA: Food photographs
SUMIKO KOBAYASHI: Editorial assistance
ATSUKO MURATA: Design
EIKO OISHI: Kitchen help

BASIC TIPS

These basic tips will save your time and make for the successful preparation of your snacks or meals.

Step I

1. Read recipes carefully and thoroughly.
2. Write down all necessary ingredients you need to buy.
3. Check all cooking equipment and place within reach.
4. Arrange all necessary seasonings, spices and herbs on kitchen counter or within your reach.
5. Prepare measuring cups and spoons.
6. Prepare all serving bowls, plates and platters near you. You may need to keep some serving platters warm.

Step II

1. Put comfortable clothes on and wear an apron, so that you will be psychologically ready for cooking.
2. Prepare plenty of kitchen towels and paper towels.

Step III

Hot food should be placed on warmed plate and cold food on chilled plate. Also look at the design on the plate if any before you place food on it. Place the plate so that the design faces the diner. With towel, wipe off around the rim if there are spilled bits or traces of liquid.

1. Seasonal appropriateness

Special attention should be given to the ingredients you choose. Some fresh fish and vegetables are available only at certain times of a year. Therefore, consider using seasonal ingredients which are abundant in the market.

2. Occasion

To serve a Japanese meal does not have to be so tedious. There are many one-pot dishes cooked on the table.
Consider the number of people you serve and whether you serve for festive occasions, luncheon, dinner, picnic or etc.

3. Flavor and Texture

Plan your menu with meat, fish and vegetables. Make each dish with different cooking method, such as grilled, steamed, fried, etc.

4. Color

Presentation of food is also important. Each ingredient has different flavor, texture and color. It is important to appeal to the eyes as well as to the tongue.

5. Nutrition

It helps when determining the kind of food to serve according to the diner's physical condition and age.

6. Cost

Seasonal fresh items generally mark lower prices. See the weekly specials for your menu planning.

BASIC COOKING INFORMATION

1 cup is equivalent to 240 ml in our recipes: (American cup measurement)
  1 American cup = 240 ml = 8 American fl oz
  1 British cup = 200 ml = 7 British fl oz
  1 Japanese cup = 200 ml
1 tablespoon = 15 ml   1 teaspoon = 5 ml

ABBREVIATIONS USED IN THIS BOOK

C=cup (s)   T=tablespoon (s)   t=teaspoon (s)   fl=fluid   oz=ounce (s)
lb (s)=pound (s)   ml=milliliter (s)   g=gram (s)   in=inch (es)   cm=centimeter
F=Fahrenheit   C=Celsius   doz=dozen   pkg (s)=package (s)
pt (s)=pint (s)   qt(s)=quart(s)

TABLES CONVERTING FROM U.S. CUSTOMARY SYSTEM TO METRICS

Liquid Measures

U.S. Customary system	oz	g	ml
1/16 cup = 1 T	1/2 oz	14 g	15 ml
1/4 cup = 4 T	2 oz	60 g	59 ml
1/2 cup = 8 T	4 oz	115 g	118 ml
1 cup = 16 T	8 oz	225 g	236 ml
1 3/4 cups	14 oz	400 g	414 ml
2 cups = 1 pint	16 oz	450 g	473 ml
3 cups	24 oz	685 g	710 ml
4 cups	32 oz	900 g	946 ml

Liquid Measures

Japanese system	oz	ml
1/8 cup	7/8 oz	25 ml
1/4 cup	1 3/4 oz	50 ml
1/2 cup	3 1/2 oz	100 ml
1 cup	7 oz	200 ml
1 1/2 cups	10 1/2 oz	300 ml
2 cups	14 oz	400 ml
3 cups	21 oz	600 ml
4 cups	28 oz	800 ml

Weights

ounces to grams*
1/4 oz = 7 g
1/2 oz = 14 g
1 oz = 30 g
2 oz = 60 g
4 oz = 115 g
6 oz = 170 g
8 oz = 225 g
16 oz = 450 g

* Equivalent

Linear Measures

inches to centimeters
1/2 in = 1.27 cm
1 in = 2.54 cm
2 in = 5.08 cm
4 in = 10.16 cm
5 in = 12.7 cm
10 in = 25.4 cm
15 in = 38.1 cm
20 in = 50.8 cm

Temperatures

Fahrenheit (F) to Celsius (C)		
freezer storage	−10°F =	−23.3°C
	0°F =	−17.7°C
water freezes	32°F =	0 °C
	68°F =	20 °C
	100°F =	37.7°C
water boils	212°F =	100 °C
	300°F =	148.8°C
	400°F =	204.4°C

Deep-Frying Oil Temperatures

300°F − 330°F (150°C − 165°C) = low
340°F − 350°F (170°C − 175°C) = moderate
350°F − 360°F (175°C − 180°C) = high

Oven Temperatures

250°F − 350°F (120°C − 175°C) = low or cool
350°F − 400°F (175°C − 204°C) = moderate or medium
400°F − 450°F (204°C − 230°C) = hot
450°F − 500°F (230°C − 260°C) = very hot

SAKE

JAPANESE
SNACKS
&
LIGHT MEALS

Yukiko Moriyama

HIJIKI (a type of sea vegetation) and ABURA-AGE

Hijiki is an excellent source of calcium and minerals.

Appetizers

1 serving INGREDIENTS

1 oz (30 g) dried *Hijiki*, a type of sea vegetation
2 slices deep-fried *tofu* (abura-age)
2T vegetable oil
4T *dashi* stock or soup stock
2T low salt soy sauce
1t *mirin*, Japanese sweet cooking wine

White toasted sesame seeds (optional)

1. Place dry *Hijiki* in a strainer and soak in water and rinse. Place in large bowl and fill the bowl half full of water.
2. Meantime dip deep fried *tofu* into hot water to remove excess oil. Pat dry with paper towel. Slice into halves lengthwise and slice into fine shreds.
3. Drain water from softened *Hijiki*. Heat oil in skillet over medium heat; add *Hijiki* and deep-fried *tofu*. Stir well while cooking; cook for 5 to 6 minutes. Add *dashi* stock, soy sauce and *mirin*. Mix well.
4. Sprinkle with toasted sesame seeds if you desire.

Appetizers

A simple way to make an ideal appetizer.

3½ oz (100 g) cuttlefish
  or squid for *sashimi**
  See preparation page
  27
½ seasoned cod fish roe
  (*tarako*)*
⅛t *sake*
*Available at the Japan-
  ese grocery store.

1. Remove thin membrane from both sides of cuttlefish.
2. Wipe off remaining membrane. Cut into thin slices.
3. Press out cod fish roe from bag; sprinkle with *sake*.
4. Mix sliced cuttle fish and cod roe.

COLORFUL TRIO SALAD

This combination of yam, *natto* and *okura* is a very nutritious appetizer.

Appetizers

2 servings INGREDIENTS

3½ oz (100 g) mountain yam
1¾ oz (50 g) *Natto*, fermented soy beans
2 *Okura* vegetable, a kind of Japanese small fuzzy mild green chili

1. Peel mountain yam and grate. Should be very sticky.
2. Mix a small amount of soy sauce and mustard with *natto*.
3. Wash and dry *Okura* and cut into ¼ in. (5 mm) thick rounds.
4. Place grated yam in a small bowl; place *natto* and *Okura* on top.

Fresh yam provides memorable texture and flavor.

Appetizers

1 serving INGREDIENTS

3½ oz (100 g) Japanese yam
⅓ oz (10 g) seasoned cod roe with chili*
1½T mayonnaise
Some *nori* seaweed (optional), shredding
*Available at the Oriental store.

1. Peel yam and cut into 1 in. (2.5 cm) square cubes.
2. Squeeze out cod roe from the bag and mix with mayonnaise. Mix with yam. Sprinkle shredded *nori* seaweed, if desired.

GRATED *DAIKON* RADISH WITH SALMON ROE, *NAMEKO* AND SARDINES

These salads may be served as accompaniments for drinks.

1. Place *shiso* leaves in a bowl. Place grated *daikon* radish on top of leaves in a small bowl. Top with salmon roe.

Garnish with lemon slices.

1. Peel and grate *daikon*. Rinse *nameko* mushrooms to remove excess water. Drain.
2. Place grated *daikon* radish in a small serving bowl. Add *nameko* mushrooms on top. Garnish with *daikon* radish sprouts.

1. Blanch white *shirasu* fish in boiling water. Drain.
2. Place grated *daikon* radish in a small bowl; place *shirasu* fish on top. Serve with soy sauce if you desire.

Appetizers

1 serving INGREDIENTS

—SALMON ROE—
2T grated *daikon* radish
1t prepared salmon roe*
2 *shiso* leaves*
1 or 2 lemon slices
*Available at the Japanese grocery store.

—NAMEKO—
2¼ in. (6cm) long *daikon* radish
2T *nameko* mushrooms
Daikon radish sprouts

—SARDINES—
2T grated *daikon* radish
2T *Shirasu Boshi*, a kind of young sardines

MOZUKU, SEA VEGETABLE SALAD

The flavor is enhanced with rice vinegar dressing.

1. Wash and rinse salted *mozuku*, sea vegetable several times to remove salty taste. Drain.
2. Mix all dressing ingredients; shake well.
3. Serve *Mozuku* in a small bowl. Top with a quail egg or shaved bonito flakes. Serve with Ponzu, Vinegar dressing.

Appetizers

1 serving INGREDIENTS

1¾ oz (50g) *Mozuku*, sea vegetable*
Ponzu, Vinegar Dressing:
2T apple vinegar or rice vinegar
2T soy sauce
2T *dashi* stock or water

1 quail egg or shaved dry bonito flakes
*Available at the Japanese grocery store.

Salads

Crisp cucumbers blend well with zesty dressing.

1 serving INGREDIENTS

2 Japanese cucumbers or
   1 English cucumber
½t salt
{ ½t hot bean paste
   (Chinese chili sauce)
 2t sesame oil
1T toasted sesame seeds

1. Wash and clean cucumbers. Cut cucumbers into halves lengthwise. Cut each piece into fourths crosswise {about 1¾ in. (4.5cm).}
2. Place cucumbers in a bowl; sprinkle ½t salt and leave for 15 to 20 minutes.
3. Wash and rinse excess salt. Mix hot bean paste and sesame oil; stir in cucumbers. Sprinkle sesame seeds on top.

SEAWEEDS SALAD

Seaweed makes a nourishing side dish for any meal.

Mix each of dressing ingredients separately until smooth and chill until serving time.

1. Wash and clean assorted seaweed. Soak dry *wakame* seaweed in water until soft. Drain water; chop into small pieces.
2. Arrange your favorite seaweed in a dish and serve with dressing of your choice.

Salads

1 serving INGREDIENTS

Assorted seaweed, sea vegetation plants, *wakame* kelp

Chinese Dressing:
1t soy sauce
1T rice vinegar
1/4t sesame oil
1T *miso*
1/2t sugar
1/4t hot chili oil
1/4t hot bean paste

Creamy Italian Dressing:
4T mayonnaise
1T milk
1/2T wine vinegar
1/2T Parmesan cheese

Japanese Salad Dressing:
2T white sesame seeds
2T rice vinegar
2 1/2T *dashi* stock or chicken stock
1 1/2T white *miso*
1/4t sugar

***Wasabi*, Horseradish Dressing:**
2T mayonnaise
1/2t *Wasabi* paste*
1t rice vinegar
*Available at the Japanese grocery store.

CRISPY *DAIKON* RADISH SALAD

The flavor of pickled plums and apple vinegar define this salad dressing.

1. Remove seeds from pickled plums. Remove outer skin. Mix with sugar, vinegar, soy sauce, salt and pepper to make paste.
2. Add oil and shake well.

Salads

2 servings INGREDIENTS

2 1/4 in. (6 cm) long *daikon* radish
1/6 oz (5 g) shaved dried bonito flakes

1. Peel *daikon* and cut into 1/4 in. (0.5 cm) thick slices; cut slices into 1/4 in. (0.5 cm) strips. Soak in ice cold water; drain well.

Plum Salad Dressing:
Makes for two servings
1/2t sugar
2 large pickled plums (*umeboshi*)
4T apple or fruit vinegar or grated apple
1t soy sauce
2/3 C vegetable oil
1/8t salt
Pepper

Salads

A delicately flavored salad dressing provides seafood with norishment.

Assorted cooked seafood such as shrimp, cuttle fish, octopus, geoduck, scallop or other shell fish

Lettuce
Horseradish sprouts

Salad Dressing:
1/3 C olive oil or vegetable oil
1T wine vinegar
1/2 clove garlic, crushed
1/2 t salt
1/4 t Dijon mustard
Dash pepper

Mix all dressing ingredients and shake well. Serve with Seafood salad.

Salads

This salad can be served as a delightful vegetarian dish.

2 romaine lettuce leaves
4 fish sticks, crab meat flavored
1 tomato
1/2 Japanese cucumber

1/4 lemon

Salad Dressing:
Makes 1C
1/4 C plain yogurt
1/4 C mayonnaise
1/2 Japanese cucumber
1/2 T lemon juice
1t fresh dill, chopped or
   1/4 t dried dill
1/4 t chili pepper

1. Mix yogurt with mayonnaise. Chop cucumber into small pieces.
2. Add chopped cucumber, lemon juice, fresh dill and chili pepper to yogurt mixture; stir and chill.

Arrange lettuce leaves and fish sticks on a plate and serve with the dressing.

ONION SALAD

Onion and bonito flakes are a wonderful combination.

1 serving INGREDIENTS

1 medium size onion

Salad Dressing:
2T low-salt soy sauce
1½T rice vinegar

Bonito flakes

1. Cut onion in half. Slice very thin. Soak in cold water with several ice cubes. Drain.
2. Place in a salad bowl; sprinkle bonito flakes. Serve with the dressing.

Salads

Serve as a side dish with your favorite entrée.

1 lb (450 g) potatoes
3 slices bacon
4T chopped onion
1t sugar
½T salt
½t all-purpose flour
Dash of pepper
1½T wine vinegar
1T minced parsley

WINE VINEGAR

Comes in red and white. Use a good imported brand of vinegar for best result.

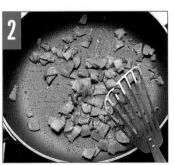

1. Scrub potatoes in cold water. Peel with vegetable peeler, or remove skin after potatoes and cooked.
2. In saucepan over high heat, cook potatoes in enough salted water to cover and boil for about 20 minutes or until tender.
3. Let cool slightly for easy handling. Cut into small cubes. Chop bacon and onion.
4. Cook bacon in a skillet over medium heat until bacon is crispy. Drain on paper towels to remove excess grease. Sauté chopped onion with bacon grease in a skillet for 3 to 4 minutes.
5. Add sugar, salt, flour and dash of pepper.
6. Add wine vinegar; stir and add potatoes and bacon.
7. Serve potatoes and sprinkle parsley on top while still hot.

MICROWAVE METHODS
Pierce potato skin in two to three places with a fork. Place potatoes in oven, arranging 3 or more like the spoke on a wheel, 1 in. (2.5 cm) apart. Cook on HIGH 8 to 9 minutes. Turn potatoes and cook another 2 minutes. For bacon, place bacon between two layers of paper towels and cook on HIGH for 1 to 1½ minutes.

CABBAGE KIM-CHEE

Kim-chee is Korea's most traditional condiment.

SALTED FISH ENTRAILS

Fish entrails are salted and used as an essential ingredient of Kim-chee. When added to the salted vegetables in fermented process, it produces vitamin B12.

Salads

4 to 6 servings INGREDIENTS

1 head Chinese cabbage
  (8lb, 3.6kg)
1C salt

garlic
1T grated fresh gin-
  ger root

Marinade:

Ⓐ
1C *dashi* stock or
  chicken stock
2t all purpose flour
1½T salted opossum
  shrimp or anchovy
  sauce

Ⓑ
1 bunch chives, cut
  into 1½ in. (4cm)
  length
1 green onion, finely
  chopped
3T ground chili pepper
3½T sugar
1T grated or crushed

1. Discard outer leaves. Cut in half.
2. Make a slit at root end, pull apart each half. If using small cabbage, cut in half.
3. Sprinkle salt between leaves, heavily over root side.
4. Put cabbage in a plastic bag, tightly secured at the top. Keep in a refrigerator overnight.
5. Rinse in water; drain and set aside 30 minutes.
6. In a small pan, heat Ⓐ ingredients to boiling, stirring constantly. When forming a paste, remove from heat; cool. When completely cooled, add Ⓑ ingredients and mix well.

7. Spread marinade paste between leaves. Grease your hand with sesame oil or wear plastic or rubber groves to prevent irritation caused by the chili pepper.
8. Folding each section in two, pack in rectangular container. Cover with plastic wrap, keep in cold and dark place. Moisture comes out in 2–3 days, but do not take out at this point. Leave a further 3–4 days at least.

An instant KIM-CHEE base has become readily available at the Oriental supermarkets. It is useful for those who do not want any failure with homemade KIM-CHEE.

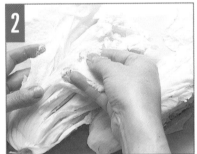

ZESTY RADISH SALAD

Chili-flavored *daikon* radish with a crispy texture.

Salads

1 to 2 servings INGREDIENTS

3¹/₄in. (8 cm) long *daikon* radish
1t salt
¹/₂ lemon, lemon peel
1¹/₄in. (3 cm) square *kombu* kelp
1 green onion, finely chopped
2 red chili peppers

Salad Dressing:
1¹/₂T rice vinegar
1T water
¹/₂T light-color soy sauce

1. Peel *daikon* and cut into quarter-rounds; cut into ¹/₄ in. (0.5cm) thick slices.
2. Sprinkle 1t salt to soften.
3. Peel lemon skin and slice into very thin strips or grate lemon peel.
4. Wipe white speckles from *kombu* kelp with towel; cut into very thin strips.
5. Cut hard stem ends from chili pepper; remove seeds and chop into small pieces.
6. Sqeeze out excess water from *daikon* radish; add lemon peel and kelp strips and chopped green onion. Mix together.
7. Mix chopped chili pepper with vinegar and pour over *daikon* radish; chili in refrigerator until serving time.

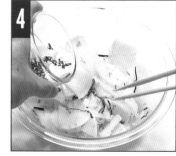

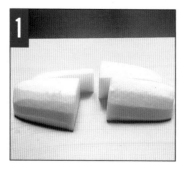

Soups

Clams are cooked in a *miso* broth.

2 bowls INGREDIENTS

1 1/2 C   *dashi* stock or chicken or vegetable stock
7 oz (200 g) small clams, *shijimi* (corbicula clams)
2 1/2 T   *miso*
Some cooking wine

1. Soak clams in salted water for several hours.
2. Wash and clean.
3. In a pot heat soup stock with clams to boiling or until clams open.
4. Put clams in small individual soup bowls.
5. Strain soup stock with cheese cloth or paper towel.
6. Add *miso* to soup stock, using strainer to make paste. Add *sake* and stir well. Heat soup stock until just before boiling point. Pour over clams. Add a small amount of soy sauce if necessary.

PORK AND KIM-CHEE SOUP

1 serving INGREDIENTS

2 oz (50 g) boneless loin
  pork
1 small potato
1/2 carrot
3/4 in. (2 cm) *daikon* radish
1/2 T vegetable oil
1 in. (2.5 cm) square fresh
  ginger root, thinly
  sliced

2 1/4 C water
Kim-chee* Hot cabbage
2T red *miso*
1 green onion, chopped

*See page 20

Pork goes well with hot-spicy vegetable pickles.

1. Remove excess fat from pork. Cut into bite size pieces.
2. Peel potato and carrot; cut into serving sizes. Cut *daikon* radish into ¼ in. (5mm) thick rounds and then quarter.
3. In a Dutch oven, heat a small amount of oil; stir-fry sliced ginger root; add pork pieces. Stir-fry until color changes; add water and vegetables. Bring to a boil. Turn heat to medium and simmer for 15 minutes, skim froth. Cook potato until *daikon* and potato are tender. Cut kim-chee into small pieces; add to the pork and vegetables. Mix *miso* and cooking stock to make paste and add to the pot. Turn off heat just before boiling point. Serve in a bowl and garnish with chopped green onion.

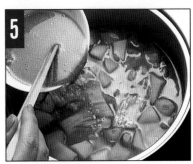

CLEAR RED SNAPPER SOUP

This soup will add a new dimension to your favorite repertoire.

Soups

2 bowls INGREDIENTS

1 large fresh red snapper head
3 in. (8 cm) leek, white part
2 C water
1 1/2 in. (3 cm) square *kombu* kelp
2T *sake*
1/2t salt

1. Pour boiling hot water over the fish head. Scrape off scales. Cut into bite size pieces.
2. Cut leek into half crosswise. Cut into fine shreds. Set aside.
3. In 3-quart pot, pour 2 C water and place *kombu* kelp and bring to a full boil. Remove *kombu* kelp and add fish. Cook over medium heat without lid on for 10 minutes. Remove scum from soup if any. Lift out fish pieces and place in large bowls. Season soup with *sake* and salt.
4. Place shredded leek on fish pieces and pour hot soup into bowls. Garnish with lemon slice or *Kinome* sprig.

CUTTLEFISH *SASHIMI*

Sashimi is an essential course in any formal dinner in Japan.

Sashimi

2 servings INGREDIENTS

- 1 whole large squid or cuttlefish
- 1 sheet *nori* seaweed
- 1/3 bunch *daikon* radish sprouts

Garnish:
Wasabi horseradish

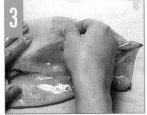

How to prepare whole squid:
1. Wash squid thoroughly under running water.
2. Place on cutting board, tail end toward you. Holding with both hands, put thumbs under "body case".
3. Push up body. Let the squid bone slip out toward you.
4. Slit body case, on bone side.
5. Hold the tail with left hand, pull tentacles and entrails out.
6. The outer skin has been removed. Cut off tough parts along edge.
7. Make very shallow cut at the edge to separate thin membrane.
8. Remove thin membrane from both sides. Wipe off remaining membrane.
9. Lay the squid fillet flat on the board, inner surface side down. With a very sharp knife score the outer surface of the squid with many shallow cuts in a crosshatch design.
10. Place bamboo mat on the board; place squid fillet and then half *nori* seaweed on top. Place *daikon* radish sprouts in center.
11. Lift bamboo mat and roll.
12. Cut in half and then cut in half again.

PICKLED MACKEREL

One of the most popular Japanese pickled dishes.

2 servings INGREDIENTS

1 whole fresh mackerel
$1/2$ C salt
$2/3$ C rice vinegar

Sashimi

. . . .

1. Remove hard scales near the tail working from tail to head. Scrape off the scales. Insert the knife behind pectoral fin and cut off head.
2. Make short slit in belly, remove entrails. Scrape out remaining entrails and blood with knife. Wash under running water.
3. Insert knife under head and slice under-belly as far as backbone. Cut the back in the same way.
4. Cut off tail. Cut off meat from back bone. Turn over and repeat.
5. Insert knife under small bones along belly. Place the fish on cutting board skin, side down.
6. With tweezers, pull out small bones along center line.
7. In large rectangular shallow dish, lay fish fillets skin sides down. Put salt on the fillets. Keep in the refrigerator overnight. Wash and rinse off salt and pat dry.
8. Place fish fillets in a dish skin side up; marinate in rice vinegar.
9. With skin side down, insert knife between skin and flesh on tail end. Pulling end of skin with left fingers, remove skin carefully. Now the fillets are ready. Slanting knife to the right, cut into $1/10$ in. (3 mm) thick slices.

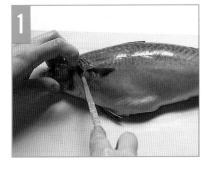

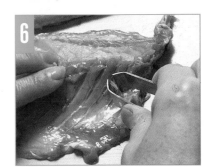

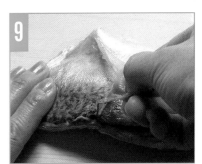

HORSE MACKEREL *SASHIMI*

This nutritious dish suits a grand party menu.

How to prepare fresh fish for *sashimi*:

1. Remove 'hard scales' from tail end.
2. Insert scissor under pectoral fin at right angle and cut off gills on both sides.
3. Slit belly to anal fin. Remove entrails and wash.
4. Insert knife through back and separate meat along backbone.
5. Turn fish over and repeat same process.
6. Now, head and skelton are one piece. Slice off small bones along belly. When cutting, work knife at right angle to fish.

7. With tweezers, pull out small bones along center line.
8. Peel back the end of skin at the head with hands. Pulling the skin with left hand while holding down fish with back of knife, peel off the skin. Peel the rest with hands (Filleted fish).
9. Chop flesh into small pieces.
10. Place the flesh on the bone. Cut *shiso* leaves into ⅜ in. (1 cm) wide strips; place on fish. Place grated ginger root and chopped green onion on top. Garnish with lemon wedge, if desired.

....

1

2

3

4

5

6

7

8

1 fresh horse mackerel or
  yellow jack
2 *shiso* leaves
1T grated fresh ginger
  root
$^{1}/_{2}$ green onion, finely
  chopped

9

10

HORSE MACKEREL ROLLED *SASHIMI*

The fish fillet turns into something special.

Sashimi

2 servings INGREDIENTS

2 horse mackerel fillets (See process on page 31)
2 *shiso* leaves, cut into 3/8 in. (1 cm) wide strips
1 in. (2.5 cm) cube fresh ginger root, cut into thin slivers.
1 sheet *nori* seaweed

1. Follow the process of making fish fillets as described on page 30.
2. Slice fillet in half, butterfly half by slicing fillet from the outer edge, part way through, to open like a book.
3. Place *nori* seaweed on a bamboo mat; place the fillets, *shiso* leaves and ginger root as shown.
4. Lift bamboo mat and roll up.
5. Cut into fourths.

STEAMED CHICKEN BREAST

Steaming

This is one of the most simple and popular chicken dishes.

2 servings INGREDIENTS

2 chicken breasts, de-boned

1t salt

1T *sake* or Chinese wine

2 anise stars

2 to 3 slices fresh ginger root

Dressing:

¼t grated garlic

1T soy sauce

½t sesame oil

¼t hot chili oil*

2T vegetable oil

Chinese coriander leaves or green onion

*Available at the Oriental store.

ANISE STAR

Brown star shaped seed with the taste of licorice. Keeps indefinitely.

1. Make short slanting slits on skin to prevent shrinkage; rub ½t salt into chicken skin. Soak anise stars in *sake* for 5 minutes.

2. Place chicken on large platter; place sliced ginger root and anise stars. Sprinkle with some *sake*.

3. Prepare steamer; place on platter and steam for 10 minutes over high heat or until chicken is no longer pink. Allow to cool. Slice chicken into serving pieces. Serve on plate. Top with coriander leaves.

4. Heat 2T oil until hot: pour over chicken.

5. Mix all dressing ingredients; pour over the chicken.

CHILLED SZECHWAN STYLE CHICKEN

This is a marvelous chicken dish.

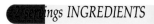

2 servings INGREDIENTS

10½ oz (300 g) chicken breasts, deboned and skinned
½t cooking wine
Some salt and pepper

2 lettuce leaves

Salad Dressing:
Makes about 1 cup
⅓ C rice vinegar
⅓ C soy sauce
2½T sugar
1t sesame oil
¼t to ½t hot chili paste
½t grated fresh ginger root
½t grated garlic

1. Place chicken breasts on a platter; sprinkle with cooking wine, salt and pepper. Steam for 20 minutes over high heat. Allow to cool. Place in a refrigerator until serving time.
2. Mix all salad dressing ingredients.
3. Slice chilled chicken breasts into thin diagonal slices; place on lettuce leaves. Serve with dressing.

HOT BEAN PASTE

A hot sauce made from broad beans, chili peppers and sometimes garlic. Comes in cans or jars. Refrigerated, keeps indefinitely in tightly sealed jars. Degree of hotness may vary between different brands.

STEAMED WONTON (SIU MAI)

Steaming

Served as an appetizer or with drinks.

Makes 24 INGREDIENTS

24 Siu Mai wrappers
Filling:
10 oz (300g) shrimp, shelled and deveined
2 *nappa* cabbage leaves
2T finely chopped green onion
1½T soy sauce
1T *sake*
1t ginger juice
1T sesame oil
1t cornstarch
24 cooked peas

1. Chop shrimp until smooth.
2. Mix rest of all ingredients; add to chopped shrimp. Stir and mix well until mixture becomes sticky.
3. Place 2t filling in center of wrapper.
4. Hold wrapper by finger circle and squeeze into round. Flatten bottom. Repeat. Or hold top edge as shown.
5. Coat steamer rack with thin film of oil. Place wontons leaving a small space in between. Steam about 12 to 14 minutes over high heat.

STEAMED CODFISH

Fresh cod fillet is the tasty key to this dish.

Steaming

1 serving INGREDIENTS

1 small slice codfish fillet
   or white meat fish
1/3 bunch *enoki* mush-
   rooms
1 fresh *shiitake* mushroom
1 mild green chili
1t light-color soy sauce
1/2t *mirin*, Japanese sweet
   cooking wine
1/8t *sake*

Alminum foil 10 in (25 cm)
   × 6 in. (15 cm)

1. Place fish fillet in center of foil.
2. Cut off hard stem ends of *Enoki* mushrooms and cut in half. Arrange mushrooms around the fillet. Cut hard stem end of *shiitake* mushroom and cut into half. Place them around the fish. Add green chili also.
3. Fold to seal foil and make a boat shape.
4. Fill skillet with about 1 in. (2.5 cm) water; bring to a boil. Place the foil wrapped fish and steam for 10 minutes or until fish is flaky and vegetables are tender.

Steaming

It is simple to make, yet very nutritious and elegant.

1 serving INGREDIENTS

3 Japanese eggplants
Some bonito flakes

Dressing:
1 1/2T soy sauce
1/2t sesame oil
1/2T rice vinegar
1/2t 7-spice powder
1/2t grated fresh ginger root
1/2t *mirin*, Japanese cooking wine

1. Cut eggplants in half lengthwise. Remove stems.
2. With the point of knife, score each eggplant 1/8 in. (5 mm) deep lengthwise. Each cut should start as just below the stem and extend to the bottom.
3. Steam eggplants for 6 to 7 minutes over high heat. Let stand to cool; keep in refrigerator until serving time. Serve with the dressing. Sprinkle bonito flakes on top.

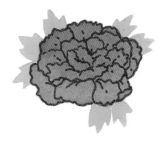

CHICKEN WITH ORANGE JUICE

This low in calorie, high in protein dish can be served as a main meal.

Simmering

5 oz (150 g) chicken thigh, deboned
½ C orange juice
1T (20 g) butter or margarine
Some *sake* or cooking wine
Some chopped scallions for topping

1. In skillet, cook chicken thigh over medium heat until light brown.
2. Add about 2T *sake*; steam for 3 minutes with lid on over low heat.
3. Add butter and season with salt and pepper to taste.
4. Sprinkle with chopped scallion.

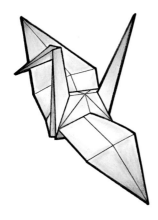

SIMMERED FISH WITH *DAIKON* RADISH

Simmering

Quick and easy way to make an elegant dish for calorie cautious people.

2 servings INGREDIENTS

1 slice yellowtail, or other fish fillet such as horse mackerel, cod, orange roughy

$1/4 - 1^1/_2$ in. (3 cm – 4 cm) *daikon* radish

$2^1/_2$ C water

1T *sake* or cooking wine

Simmering Broth:

2 C water

1T *sake*

1T *mirin*, Japanese sweet cooking wine

2T light-color soy sauce

1 in. (2.5 cm) square fresh ginger root

$1/_2$t salt

1. Peel *daikon*; cut in half lengthwise and cut into quarter-rounds.
2. In a saucepan, cook *daikon* in $2^1/_2$ C water and 1T *sake* until tender.
3. Pour boiling water over the fish fillet to remove fish odor.
4. In a large pot, place cooked *daikon* and fish fillet; add simmering broth. Cook on high until boil. Skim off froth and reduce heat to low, placing foil on it. Add $1/_2$t salt if necessary.

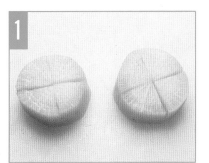

PORK *SUKIYAKI*

One of the most popular Japanese dishes.

Simmering

1 to 2 servings INGREDIENTS

3$\frac{1}{2}$ oz (100 g) pork loin
5 oz (140 g) *Shirataki* fimaments or bean threads, softened
12 oz (300 g) firm *tofu*
1$\frac{3}{4}$ oz (50 g) onion, chopped
1$\frac{3}{4}$ oz (50 g) chinese nappa cabbage
1 green onion
Simmering broth:
$\frac{1}{2}$C plus 1T soup stock
1T soy sauce
1T *mirin,* Japanese sweet cooking wine
1T *sake*
1T sugar

1. Cut pork loin into small serving sizes.
2. Rinse *shirataki* filaments (yam noodles) or soak dry bean threads in water to soften. Cut into small pieces.
3. Chop green onion.
4. Bring simmering stock to a boil in a pot; add pork, filaments, and onion. Cut *tofu* into 1 in. (2.5 cm) cubes; add to the broth. Simmer over medium heat, skimming froth, for 15 minutes.

Simmering

This dish is full of tasty ingredients.

1 serving INGREDIENTS

1³/₄ oz (50g) pork loin, thin slices
7 oz (200g) potatoes
1³/₄ oz (50g) onion
1³/₄ oz (50g) *shirataki* filaments
Some snow peas or green beans

Cooking Broth:
1C cooking broth, soup stock
3T soy sauce
1T *mirin*, Japanese sweet cooking wine
1T *sake*
2t sugar

1. Cut pork into small pieces.
2. Skin potatoes and cook until done. Cut into small bite-size pieces.
3. Chop onion.
4. Parboil *shirataki* filaments and chop roughly.
5. Cook beans and set aside.

1. In 2-quart sauce pan, add all cooking broth ingredients; bring to a boil. Add potatoes, pork, onion, *shirataki* filaments; cook over medium heat until potatoes are tender. Skim froth during cooking.

ORIENTAL PORK POT ROAST

Slow cooking makes the meat tender.

Simmering

INGREDIENTS

10½ oz (300 g) boneless
   pork loin roast
1 in. (2.5 cm) square fresh
   ginger root, 5–6 slices
1 Anise star*
3½ C water

Simmering broth:
⅔ C stock from cooked
   pork
1T sake
1t sugar
½T mirin, Japanese sweet
   cooking wine

2T soy sauce
Garnish and condiment:
green onion
mustard

*Available at the Oriental
   store.

1. Cut pork into large chunks.
2. In a Dutch oven or 3-quart sauce pan, place pork, sliced
ginger root, anise star and water; bring to a full boil over high
heat. Partially cover the pot.
Turn heat to low and simmer about 30 minutes. Skim off froth
during cooking. Let sit to cool.
3. Rinse pork under running water. Strain cooking broth, or
leave in a refrigerator over night and remove hard fat.
4. In 3-quart sauce pan, cook pork with simmering broth
over medium heat for 20 minutes, placing alminum foil over
the meat in the pot.
5. Add 2T soy sauce; cook 30 minutes longer over low heat.
6. Slice green onion 1½ in. (4 cm) long fine shreds. Place
over cooked pork and serve with mustard.

Make a large portion for later use. It can be kept in a refrigerator for 4 to 5 days.

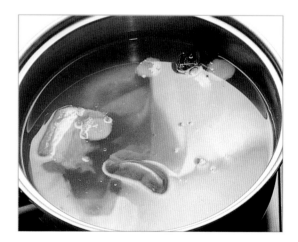

Simmering

Carrot adds a bright touch of color and mellow flavor to this dish.

2 servings **INGREDIENTS**

5 oz (150 g) beef tripe
¼ small carrot
½ block *konnyaku* (yam jelly)
¼ block firm *tofu*
1 in. (2.5 cm) cube fresh ginger root, sliced thin
1½ C water
3T *miso*
½t sugar

Garnish:
1T chopped green onion

1. In a 2-quart sauce pan, place tripe, sliced ginger root and 2C water; bring to a full boil over high heat. Discard cooking broth; set aside.
2. Cut carrot, *konnyaku* and *tofu* into serving size pieces; cook with 1½C water until carrot is tender. Add tripe. Mix *miso*, sugar and with 2T cooking broth; pour over tripe. Stir well. Garnish with chopped green onion.

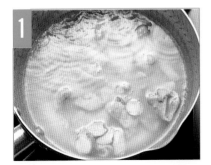

YOSENABE FISH HOT POT

A rich variety of shellfish and fish is cooked in a broth.

2–3 servings INGREDIENTS

Fish: salmon, cod, shrimp, scallop, crab or other seafoods of your choice
1 leek or 1 bunch green onion
1 can 5 oz (75 g) *shirataki* filaments or 2 oz (60 g) bean threads
3–4 *Nappa* cabbage leaves
1/2 bunch chrysanthemum leaves or spinach leaves
1 *shiitake* mushroom, *shimeji*, *enoki* mushrooms
Some *daikon* radishes, carrots, trefoil
1 block firm *tofu*, well drained

Cooking broth:
5 C *dashi* stock or *kombu* kelp 2 in. (5 cm) square plus 7 C water
1 1/2 t salt
2 T light-color soy sauce
1 T *sake* or cooking wine

Garnishes:
Finely chopped scallion
Grated *daikon* radish with chili *Ponzu*, lime juice
Grated plain *daikon* radish
Lemon juice

1. Wipe *kombu* kelp dry with kitchen towel to remove white spots. Place kelp in a large pot and add 5–6 C water; bring to a boil uncovered. Turn off heat and remove the kelp.
2. Cut green onion diagonally and parboil *shirataki* filaments. Chop. Cut *nappa* cabbage into 4 or 5 pieces. Soften *shiitake* mushroom and cut off stems and cut into halves. Cut off hard stem ends of *shimeji* or *enoki* mushrooms.
3. Cut *tofu* into small bite size pieces.
4. Place each of ingredients into earthen pot; pour in hot simmering stock and cook ingredients. Serve with garnishes of your choice.

ODEN, FISH CAKE CASSEROLE

Simmering

This nourishing dish is one of Japan's most popular.

2 to 4 servings INGREDIENTS

Assorted fish cake products:
Fried *tofu* patties
Deep-fried *tofu*
Steamed fish paste cake (*kamaboko*)
Yam jelly (*konnyaku*)
Deep-fried fish balls
Kombu kelp
Grilled fish paste rolls (*chikuwa*)
Stuffed deep-fried *tofu* pouches
cabbage rolls
Other vegetables such as *daikon* radish, carrot.

Simmering Broth:
4 C *dashi* stock, fish based stock
A pinch of salt
3T light-color soy sauce
1T *sake,* Japanese wine
$1/2$T sugar

Condiments:
Mustard
7-spice powder

PREPARATION
Cut each fish product into serving sizes. Blanch deep-fried fish cakes in boiling water to remove excess oil. Peel *daikon*, carrot and or potato if you prefer. Cut *daikon* into 3/4 in. (2 cm) rounds or half moons. Cut carrot into $1/2$ in. (1.5 cm) rounds. Cook vegetables in boiling water until tender.
In a large flame-proof earthen-ware pot, or slow cooker, heat *dashi* stock, fish stock to simmering; add salt, soy sauce, wine and sugar.
Add assorted fish cakes and simmer over a very low heat. You can cook with lid or without depending on the type of pot you use. Some fish products should almost float and by the time they are ready to serve, simmering stock maybe reduced by $1/3$ at least, so be sure to use enough stock at the beginning.
This dish can be served at the table for everyone to help yourself.

GRILLED SALMON STEAK

A special recipe transforms the salmon fillet into a delicacy.

Grilling

2 servings INGREDIENTS

2 salmon steaks
2T butter or margarine
⌠ 1t salt
⌡ ½t grated lemon peel

½ bunch spinach

1. Wash and clean spinach. Cut off stem ends; cut into ½ in. (4 cm) lengths.
2. Melt 1T butter in a skillet over medium heat. Cook salmon steaks until both sides are light brown, turning once. Place on a serving plate. Season with salt and grated lemon peel mixture.
3. Melt 1T butter in a skillet, sauté spinach over medium heat for a few minutes. Serve with salmon steaks.

Grilling

This dish has a tasty and exotic Oriental flavor.

1 serving INGREDIENTS

1 fresh horse mackerel or
    trout
Salt

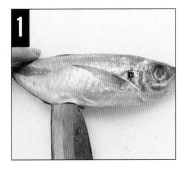

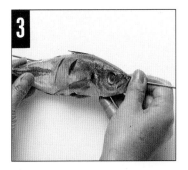
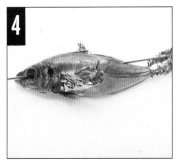

1. Remove hard scales from tail end toward head.

2. Lift pectoral fin and cut off.

3. Place fish head to the right and make a short slit just under fin. Scrape out entrails with care so that shape will be retained. Wash thoroughly under running water. Pat dry with paper towels. Make slanting slits on both sides.

4. Hold fish; insert skewer just below eye, under bone, bringing the tip out just below the gill flap. Tail will stand erect if skewer is made to come through about 2 in. (5 cm) from the end of the tail on the same side that the skewer was inserted. The skewer should go in and come out of the same side of the fish. Repeat with other skewer.

5. Sprinkle fish lightly with salt.

6. Wrap tail and fins with foil.

7. For best results, grill the side that will face up on a plate until about 60% cooked. Turn and grill the back side until cooked. Remove foil after placing on a plate.

BROILED-*TERIYAKI* YELLOW TAIL

This marinade sauce can be used with meat.

Grilling

1 serving INGREDIENTS

1 yellow tail fillet

Marinade Sauce:
1T *mirin,* Japanese sweet
   cooking wine
1½T soy sauce
1t *sake*

1. Marinate fish fillet in marinade sauce for 20 minutes.
2. Broil over charcoal fire or in oven. Baste occasionally while broiling. For pan-frying, heat 1T vegetable oil in a skillet over medium heat; cook fish fillet, turning once. Remove the fillet to a plate. Cook remaining sauce in a skillet and pour over fillet.

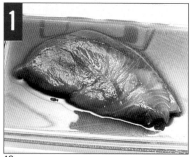

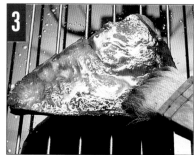

BROILED SMALL FISH

Grilling

Served as a side dish or with drinks.

2 servings INGREDIENTS

Broil both sides and garnish with lemon wedges.

6 small sun-dried fish, sardines, smelt or nese *SHISHAMO**
*Available at Japanese grocery store.

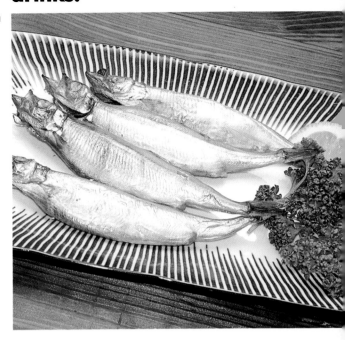

BARBECUED MEAT

Broiling

A special marinade transforms the meat into a mouthwatering delicacy.

2 servings INGREDIENTS

Beef, chicken, spareribs or other meat of your choice

Marinade Sauce A:
Makes enough for
  1 pound of meat
2¹/₂T soy sauce
1T sugar
1¹/₂T sesame oil
1T *mirin* Japanese sweet cooking wine
1t toasted sesame seeds
1 clove garlic, crushed
2T chopped green onion
¹/₂t *sake*

Mix all ingredients.
Marinade Sauce B:
(Hot-Spicy Sauce)
Makes 2 cups
4T each, red and white *miso*
1 clove garlic, crushed
¹/₂ scallion, minced
2¹/₂T sesame seed oil
¹/₂T chili pepper
1C soy sauce
2T hot Korean sauce, KOCHU JAN
1t grated and squeezed fresh ginger juice
¹/₄ apple, grated
¹/₄C each *sake* and *mirin*
2¹/₂T water
6T sugar

TERIYAKI CHICKEN

One of the best known and the most popular chicken dishes.

4 servings INGREDIENTS

Assoortment of chicken wings, thighs, liver, giblets, ground chicken meat balls

Barbecue Sauce:
$1/2$ C *mirin*, Japanese sweet cooking wine
$1/2$ C soy sauce
1 T sugar

Garnishes:
Sansho powder
7-spice powder
lemons

Variation:
Pork, pineapple, tomato, green peppers

1. In a small saucepan, add all sauce ingredients; cook over medium low heat until thickened. Let cool slightly. Baste sauce over meat while grilling.

VARIATION
Barbecue Sauce:
$2^{1}/_{2}$ T vegetable oil
1 t salt
1 clove garlic, crushed
$1/4$ C pineapple juice
$1/3$ C brown sugar
1 T red wine vinegar
1 T soy sauce
Skewer pork, pineapple, tomato and green pepper. Brush with sauce.
Grill until done, basting once or twice.

Broiling

Garlic enhances the flavor of this steak.

3$\frac{1}{2}$ oz–4 oz (100 g to 120 g) sirloin steak
Salt and pepper
$\frac{1}{2}$T butter

Marinade Sauce:
1T soy sauce
1t *mirin,* Japanese sweet cooking wine
1 clove garlic, minced
1 in. (2.5 cm) square ginger root, grated

1. Cut off excess fat from meat. Lightly season with salt and pepper. Cut into small bite size pieces. Marinate in sauce for 30 minutes.
2. Melt butter in a skillet; cook meat over high heat.
3. Pour in leftover marinade sauce in a skillet and turn off heat.

This colorful dish is pleasantly arranged.

Grilling

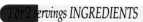

1 or 2 servings INGREDIENTS

2 fresh asparagus stalks
2 lean bacon slices
1t vegetable oil

1. Steam or cook asparagus until tender. Immerse in water.
2. Wrap bacon strip around an asparagus stalk and secure end with tooth pick.

3. Heat oil in skillet; sauté asparagus for several minutes over medium heat or until bacon is crispy.
4. Drain on paper towels. Remove tooth pick and cut into halves.

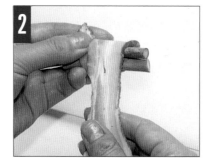

Pan-frying

Elegant enough to be served as a main course.

2 Japanese eggplants
4 thin sliced pork meat
1T vegetable oil
1t chopped fresh ginger root
1 clove garlic, chopped

Cooking Broth:
1t *mirin*, Japanese sweet cooking wine
1T soy sauce
1t salt
1C *dashi* stock or chicken broth
1t cornstarch plus 1t water

1. Cut stems off from tip of eggplants. With sharp knife, score each eggplant 1/8 in. (5mm) deep lengthwise.
Soak in water. Wipe eggplants dry.
2. Cut eggplants in half lengthwise. Each cut should start at just below the stem and extend to the bottom.
3. Place two pieces of pork between the slashed eggplant.
4. Heat skillet over medium heat, add chopped ginger and garlic; stir-fry until aroma comes out. Add eggplants and cook all sides until lightly browned.
4. In medium saucepan, mix all cooking broth ingredients; heat the broth over medium heat. Add lightly browned eggplants. Cook for 4 to 5 minutes over medium heat.
5. Add mixed cornstarch and water. Cook until thickened.

TOFU ITALIAN

This enchanting combination of *tofu* and Parmesan cheese can be served as a light lunch.

Grilling

2 servings INGREDIENTS

1 block firm *tofu* (12 oz to 16 oz), well drained
1t grated fresh ginger root
1T soy sauce
All purpose flour for dusting *tofu*
1T butter
1T Parmesan cheese
1T vegetable oil or butter

● PIZZA SAUCE

Ready made pizza sauce is available in different sizes and ingredients.

1. Marinate *tofu* in soy sauce and grated ginger root for a few minutes. Drain excess soy sauce. Lightly coat *tofu* with flour. Dip into beaten egg and Parmesan cheese mixture.
2. In a skillet, heat oil; add *tofu* and fry on both sides until golden brown. Serve hot with condiments of your choice.

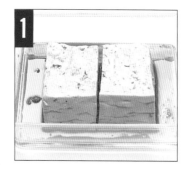

Pan-frying

Cheese filling makes a colorful contrast.

1 serving INGREDIENTS

2 *Hanpen* fish cakes, spongy
   fish cake product
Some shredded mozarella
   cheese
Some all-purpose flour
1T butter or margarine
1t soy sauce

1. Cut fish cakes into halves diagonally into triangular pieces. Make slit on a longer side of each cake.
2. Stuff shredded cheese into slit of cake, about 1 heaping T. Coat fish cake with flour.
3. Melt butter in skillet over low heat; add fish cakes. Cook cakes until cheese melts and fish cakes are lightly browned.
4. Remove from skillet. Add 1t soy sauce into skillet. Pour over fish cakes.

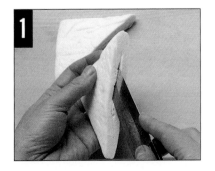

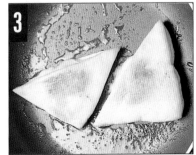

JAPANESE OMELET

A simple omelet can be turned into an elegant side dish.

Pan-frying

2 servings INGREDIENTS

3 eggs
$^2/_3$ oz (20g) *Shirasu* fish (young small sardines)
$^2/_3$ oz (20g) onion
2 to 3T butter or margarine

Garnishes: **Condiments:**
Lettuce   Ketchup
Cucumber   Mayonnaise
Parsley
Lemon

1. Chop onion. Melt 1T butter in an omelet pan or skillet; add onion and cook until transparent. Season with salt and pepper. Add *Shirasu* fish and stir-fry for 2 to 3 minutes over medium heat. Let stand to cool.

2. Beat 3 eggs in a bowl; add cooled *Shirasu* fish and stir.

3. Melt 2T butter in an omelet pan or skillet, pour egg mixture, and cook until surface is half settled. Gently fold the omelet with spatula. Slide omelet onto a warmed plate and add garnish of your choice.

Pan-frying

Assorted fillings make a colorful contrast.

2 servings INGREDIENTS

2 eggs
1 small tomato, chopped
½ green pepper, chopped
1T onion, chopped

¼t salt
2 slices bacon, chopped into small pieces
1t olive oil

1. Cook bacon in skillet over medium heat. Drain on paper towel. Set aside.
2. Heat 1t olive oil in skillet over medium heat; add tomato, green pepper and onion; stir-fry 2 minutes.

3. Pour in beaten eggs; tilt pan to coat bottom. Cook till top is set and underside is just browned.
4. Fold omelet over in half of the cooked omelet with a spatula and gently fold the other half over.

GRILLED DEEP-FRIED *TOFU*

Calcium rich *tofu* can be served at any meal.

Grilling

....

ngs INGREDIENTS

2 deep-fried *tofu*
2T grated bonito flakes

1. Pour hot boiling water over deep-fried *tofu* to remove excess grease.
2. Grill *tofu* on both sides or bake in 375°F (190°C) oven for 5 minutes.
3. Cut into fourths, then cut into triangle shapes. Or cut into serving sizes.
4. Sprinkle bonito flakes on top. Serve with soy sauce.

EGGPLANT WITH CHEESE

Microwave Cooking

Eggplants are widely used in many countries, and this is my favorite version.

1 serving INGREDIENTS

- 2 Japanese eggplants
- 1 small potato
- 1T chopped parsley
- Some shredded mozarella cheese
- 1T vegetable oil
- 1t salt
- Dash pepper
- 2T spaghetti sauce

1. Cut eggplants into halves lengthwise. Make shallow slits diagonally on skin. Soak in water. Drain on paper towel. Set aside.
2. Peel potato and slice into thin rounds.
3. Heat vegetable oil in skillet over medium heat; add eggplant and cook until both sides lightly brown. Sprinkle with 1t salt. Set aside. aside.
4. Place potato slices in baking dish. Cover with plastic wrap and microwave for 2 minutes on HIGH.
5. Season with salt and pepper to taste; cover with spaghetti sauce. Add cooked eggplants.
6. Sprinkle shredded cheese and parsley on top. Cover with plastic wrap and microwave for 2 minutes on HIGH.

GROUND BEEF CUP WITH VEGETABLES

6 oz (150 g) frozen mixed
vegetables

4T shredded mozarella
cheese

10½ oz (300 g) ground
lean beef

½ package onion soup
mix

1 egg, beaten

⅓ C bread crumbs

1T ketchup

This hearty meat dish is enhanced with mozzarella cheese.

1. Cook, covered, frozen mixed vegetables in microwave oven for 2 minutes on HIGH.
2. Stir in 2T cheese. Divide into fourths.
3. Mix ground beef, onionsoupmix, beaten egg, bread crumbs and ketchup. Divide into fourths.
4. In a small oven proof dish, place ground beef mixture as shown. Fill the beef cup with vegetable and cheese mixture.
5. Place cups in a microwave oven. Arrange like the spokes on a wheel, 1 in. (2.5 cm) apart.
6. Cook on HIGH for 6 minutes. When half the cooking time has elapsed, rearrange position. Sprinkle cheese on top.
7. Cook another 2 minutes on HIGH. Place waxed paper on cheese and let it stand for 2 to 3 minutes.

ORANGE FLAVORED FISH

The secret of this dish is orange juice.

1 slice white fish fillet, cod
  or red snapper
1t butter or margarine
$^1/_4$t grated orange peel
1T orange juice
$^1/_2$t *Teriyaki* Sauce (or
  mixture of soy sauce
  and *mirin*)
1 scallion, chopped
$^1/_4$t grated fresh ginger
  root

1. Place fish fillet in a baking dish.
2. In a small dish, place butter or margarine; cover with plastic wrap and microwave 10 to 15 seconds on HIGH. Stir in orange juice, *Teriyaki* Sauce, chopped scallion and grated ginger root.
3. Pour over fish. Cover with plastic wrap leaving some space for steam to escape. Microwave 3 to 4 minutes on HIGH or until done. Leave for 2 to 3 minutes with wrap on. Serve with soy sauce if desired.

Microwave Cooking

1 serving INGREDIENTS

8³/₄ oz (250 g) potato
²/₃ oz (20 g) bacon, chopped
1 oz (30 g) shredded mozzarella or Gouda cheese
Tonkatsu sauce
1 oz (30 g) onion

Can be prepared in minutes.

1. Peel potatoes; slice into thin small pieces.
2. Slice onion thin.
3. Place potatoes, bacon on a dish and add small amount of *Tonkatsu* sauce. Sprinkle with cheese.
4. Cook in microwave oven on HIGH for 2 to 3 minutes.

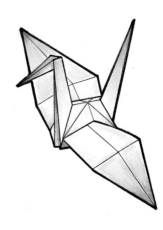

This dish is appropriate for festive occasions.

Sautéing

2 servings **INGREDIENTS**

¹/₄ pound (450g) shrimp
1 green pepper, chopped
²/₃ C bean sprouts
¹/₂ onion, sliced thin
⁵/₆ oz (25 g) sliced mushrooms
¹/₂t salt
1T vegetable oil
1t oyster sauce*
1t cornstarch plus
1t water

*Available at the Oriental
 grocery store.

1. Cut off heads of shrimp. Remove shell.
2. Heat 1T oil in wok; cook shrimp until color turns pink.
Remove from wok and set aside.
3. Stir fry green pepper, bean sprouts, onion and mushrooms
in wok over high heat until vegetables are tender.
4. Add salt and oyster sauce and stir well. Add shrimp and
cornstarch mixture to thicken.

Stir-frying

STIR-FRIED SQUID

Squid is transformed into a legendary Oriental delicacy.

2 servings INGREDIENTS

7 oz (200 g) squid, tentacles removed

1t minced fresh ginger

2T vegetable oil

Ⓐ
- 1t hot chili paste
- 1T soy sauce
- 1t *sake*
- ½t sugar

1 small green pepper, chopped

1 small red pepper or ⅓ carrot, sliced thin rounds

1t minced ginger root

½ clove garlic, chopped

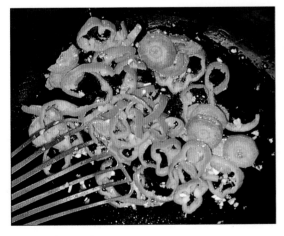

Follow instruction for cleaning squid on page 27

1. Remove thin membrane from both sides.
2. Make a shallow cut on skin.
3. In a saucepan, bring water to a boil and add 1t minced ginger root; immerse squid for a few seconds to remove fish smell.
4. Cut into slices, about ½ in. (1 cm) wide.
5. Heat 2T oil in wok over medium high heat; add garlic and ginger root to release aroma.
6. Add green pepper and carrot and stir fry for a few minutes.
7. Add Ⓐ ingredients and stir once. Add squid and stir fry for a minute.

Soy sauce and sesame oil impart a rich aroma to this dish.

2 servings INGREDIENTS

1 burdock root, about 12–15 in. (31–38 cm) long
1 small carrot
1 to 2 red chili (or 7-spice powder, 1t)
2T oil
1t sugar
½T *mirin*, Japanese sweet cooking wine
1¼T light-color soy sauce
1t rice vinegar
1t sesame oil

1. Scrape burdock root and cut into thin slivers. Soak in water for 15 minutes; drain. Scrape carrot and cut into thin slivers just like the burdock root.
2. Trim off stem ends of dried red chili peppers; remove seeds. Chop into small pieces.
3. Heat oil in skillet over medium heat; add chopped chili and stir once. Add burdock root; stir fry for a few minutes. Add carrot. Cook, stirring constantly; add sugar. Stir once. Add *mirin* and soy sauce and stir, braise vegetables for 2 to 3 minutes. Add 1T water. Stir and add rice vinegar and sesame oil and turn off heat.
Garnish with the toasted sesame seeds.

Sautéing

Try it while still hot.

2 servings INGREDIENTS

10¹/₂ oz (300 g) clams
¹/₂ T vegetable oil
1 clove garlic, minced
1 to 2T butter
1t soy sauce
1t minced parsley
1T *sake*, or cooking wine
1T lemon peel

1. Heat wok and add ¹/₂T oil; add minced garlic to release aroma.
2. Add washed and throughly cleaned clams and stir fry vigorously for a minute; add 1t soy sauce and 1T *sake* and cover to steam clams. Steam for 2 to 3 minutes or until clams open.
3. Add butter and minced parsley and stir fry until butter melts.
4. Sprinkle with lemon peel and turn off heat.

SAUTÉED ASPARAGUS

The bright green gives a pleasing color contrast to any dish.

Sautéing

1 or 2 servings INGREDIENTS

4 fresh asparagus stalks
1T butter
Pepper

1. Break off hard stem ends of asparagus stalks.
2. Cook in lightly salted boiling water for a few minutes. Immerse in cold water to retain color. Cut in half.
3. Heat butter in skillet over medium heat. Sauté cooked asparagus for a few minutes. Sprinkle with pepper.

Sautéing

This delightful recipe makes a colorful addition to a party menu.

1 serving INGREDIENTS

8³/₄ oz (250g) potatoes
1 oz (30g) pork, thin sliced and chopped
¹/₃ oz (10g) carrot
1 green pepper
²/₃ oz (20g) onion
Some curry powder
1T (10g) butter
²/₃ oz (20g) corns
Some salt to taste

Small amount of vegetable oil

1. Cook potatoes and remove skin. Cut potatoes into ¹/₈ in. (3mm) × 1¹/₈ in. (3cm) pieces.
2. Slice green pepper, onion, and carrot thin.
3. Heat skillet over medium high heat, add oil. Sauté pork until well done.
4. Add potatoes, other vegetables; stir fry untill vegetables are tender and potatoes are lightly browned.
5. Mix curry powder with a drop of water. Add to pork and vegetables. Stir once. And butter.

DEEP-FRIED POT STICKERS

These pot stickers are often served with dips.

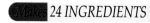
Makes 24 INGREDIENTS

24 Wonton wrappers

Filling:
14 oz (400g) *Nappa* cabbage
7 oz (200g) ground pork
1 green onion, minced
1t ginger juice
1 1/2t salt
1 1/2T soy sauce
1T *sake* or cooking wine
1T sesame oil

Oil for deep-frying

Condiment:
Tonkatsu Sauce*
or equal amount of ketch-up and soy sauce
*Available at Oriental store.

1. Cook *nappa* cabbage in salted boiling water until soft. Drain. Chop and sqeeze out excess water.
2. Mix pork with rest of all ingredients; add chopped cabbage.
3. Mix and set aside.
4. Place about 2t fillings on center of wonton wrapper. Fold in half. Press edges with fork as shown.
5. Deep-fry in 350°F (180°C) oil until light brown.

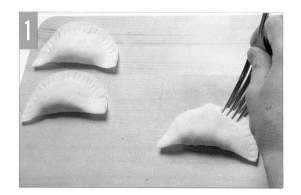

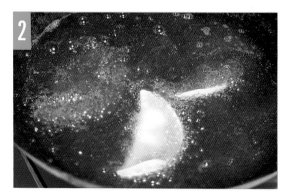

DEEP-FRIED STUFFED CHICKEN

Deep-frying

This dish is another attractive way to serve chicken.

1 to 2 servings INGREDIENTS

7 oz (200 g) deboned and skin removed chicken breast
1 package *Natto,* fermented soy beans*
2 large pickled plums
Egg Batter:
1 C all purpose flour
¼ C water to make paste
1 egg
1 T red *miso*
Tabasco sauce
*Available at the Oriental grocery store.

1. Cut chicken breast in half at the center. Butterfly each half by slicing breast from the outer edge, part way through, to open like a book.
2. Mix *natto* with a small amount of soy sauce and mustard. Remove seeds from pickled plums. Chop into small pieces.
3. Mix *natto* and chopped plums; place 1 t mixture on the chicken breast. Roll up.
4. Make egg batter; mix with *miso* and a drop of Tabasco sauce.
5. Dip rolled chicken breast into batter; deep-fry in 350°F (180°C) oil.
Drain. Cut in half if you desire.

DEEP FRIED SMELT

The crispy texture holds a delicate flavor inside.

1. Dust fresh smelts with cornstarch.
2. Heat deep-frying oil to 350°F (175°C); deep-fry smelt until light brown.
3. Place on a plate and garnish with grated ginger root.

Deep-frying

INGREDIENTS

6 smelts
Cornstarch for coating

Deep-frying oil

1t grated fresh ginger root
Soy sauce

DEEP-FRIED SARDINES

A touch of *shiso* flakes, traditional Japanese seasoning, enhances the flavor of this dish.

1. Mix flour and egg water to make thick paste. Add *shiso* flakes and mix well.
2. Heat deep-frying oil to 350°F (180°C). Dip each sardine into batter and deep-fry until light brown. Drain.

Deep-frying

INGREDIENTS

1 oz (80 g) small sardines

Batter:
All-purpose flour
Water to make paste
1T to 2T seasoned *shiso* leaves flakes (YUKARI)*
1 egg
Oil for deep-frying

Garnish:
lemon wedges
YUKARI

*Available at Japanese Grocery store.

Yukari is a mixture of dried shiso leaves and salt. Shiso, commonly known as the beefsteak plant of mint family, is used as a garnish and in pickles.

FRIED POTATOES

Deep-frying

Making your own fried potatoes is particularly fun.

2 servings INGREDIENTS

4 potatoes

Oil for deep-frying

Condiments:
Ketchup
Salt
Vinegar
Salt and grated orange or
  lemon peel mixture.

1. Peel and cut potatoes ½ in. (1 cm) thick slices; cut slices into ½ in. (1 cm) strips.
2. Heat deep-frying oil to 350°F (180°C); deep-fry potatoes until light brown. Drain. Season with salt or salt mixture.

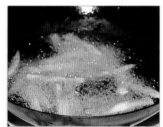

DEEP-FRIED SQUID JAPANESE STYLE

Deep-frying

This egg battered dish is one of the most popular in Japan.

1 serving INGREDIENTS

4 oz (120 g) squid ten-
  tacles
1t curry powder
Egg Batter:
  Flour
  Water to make paste
  1 egg

1. Wipe off excess water from squids. Cut into serving pieces. Dust with curry powder. In a large bowl, break egg and add flour and water to make a thick lumpy batter. Do not stir well. Dip squid into batter. Deep-fry in 375°F (190°C) oil.

CRISPY DEEP-FRIED SOLE

Sweet and sour sauce makes this dish special.

Deep-frying

INGREDIENTS

1 fresh sole
A pinch of salt
2T all-purpose flour
$1/8$t grated lemon peel

Hot *Daikon* Radish:
1T grated *daikon* radish
$1/2$t 7-spice powder

Vinegar Sauce:
1T rice vinegar
1T soy sauce

1T finely shredded cooked bamboo shoots
1T finely shredded carrot

Sweet and Sour Sauce:
Ⓐ
$2/3$C soup stock
1T soy sauce
$1^1/2$t sugar
1T rice vinegar
1t cornstarch plus
1t water

1. Scrape off scales. Cut off pectoral fin on both sides. Remove entrails carefully with tip of knife. Wash under running water and wipe dry. Rub a pinch of salt on both sides. Make one or two slit diagonally as shown above. Dust with cornstarch.
2. Heat deep-frying oil to 350°F (180°C). Slide head into oil holding tail. Deep-fry for a few minutes. Turn over and deep-fry until light brown. Serve with *daikon* radish and vinegar sauce, or sweet and sour sauce.

Heat Ⓐ ingredients until sugar dissolves. Add **cornstarch mixture and stir until thickened.** Place shredded bamboo shoots and carrot on sole and pour sauce on top.

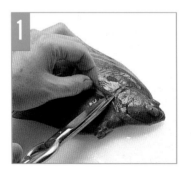

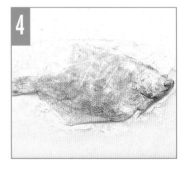

CRISPY DEEP-FRIED CHICKEN

Deep-frying

This chicken dish can be served hot or cold.

2 servings INGREDIENTS

12 oz (350g) chicken wings and thighs
4 small green chili (optional)

Marinade Sauce:
$1/2$t ginger juice from grated fresh ginger
2T soy sauce
1T cooking wine

2T to 3T cornstarch or all-purpose flour
Oil for deep-frying

Garnishes:
Lemon wedges
Sansho powder*
Mustard or ketchup
*Available at Japanese grocery store.

1. Pierce skin of chicken with a folk. Marinate in marinade sauce for 20 to 30 minutes.
2. Heat oil to 350°F (180°C). Pat dry green chili and prick chili two to three places to prevent shrinking. Deep-fry for 2 minutes.
3. Wipe off excess sauce. Dust with cornstarch and deepfry for 5 minutes or until golden brown.
4. Serve with garnishes of your choice.

POTATO CROQUETTES

This hearty potato dish is enhanced with ground chicken.

Deep-frying
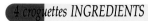

4 croquettes INGREDIENTS

6 oz–7 oz (150 g–200 g)
  ground chicken meat
1/2 minced onion
2T vegetable oil
1T salt
Dash pepper
13/4 lb (800 g) potatoes
1/2C all-purpose flour
1 egg
1C bread crumbs
Oil for deep-frying

Condiment:
Ketchup

1. Peel potatoes and cook in water until done. Test with bamboo skewer.
2. Heat 2T oil; add chopped onion and sauté until transparent. Add ground chicken and cook until done. Season with salt and pepper.
3. Mash cooked potatoes; mix with cooked chicken.
4. Divide into fourths. Make 4 patties.
5. Coat the patties with flour, beaten egg and bread crumbs. Deep-fry in oil, 340°F–360°F (170°C–180°C), until golden brown.

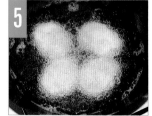

DEEP-FRIED BEEF WITH CHEESE

Deep-frying

2 servings INGREDIENTS

3¹/₂ oz (100 g) thin sliced beef
5T Grated cheddar cheese
Some *nori* seaweed flakes*

Batter:

All-purpose flour
Water
1 egg

*Available at the Japanese grocery store.

This dish has a tasty and exotic flavor.

1. Place thin sliced beef front of you. Place a small amount of grated cheese and sprinkle seaweed flakes on top. Roll up.
2. Make egg batter and dip rolled beef and deep-fry in oil, 350°F (180°C) for a few minutes. Drain.

SPRING ROLLS WITH CHICKEN AND CHEESE

This is one of the all-time international favorites.

Deep-frying
....
1 serving INGREDIENTS

6 oz (150 g) shredded
  mozarella cheese
1¾ oz (50 g) bacon
8¾ oz (250 g) chicken
  breast, deboned and
  skin removed
10 spring roll wrappers

1. Place spring wrapper front of you. Place cheese, chicken and bacon on top.
2. Fold sides into overlap. Fold sides in to overlap again. Place a small amount of flour and water mixture at top of wrapper to seal.
3. Heat deep-frying oil to 350°F (170°C to 180°C) and deep-fry rolls until golden brown. Drain. Cut in half if you desire.

1

2

Deep-frying

These nutritious spring rolls fit perfectly in a grand party menu.

10 rolls INGREDIENTS

- 10 spring roll wrappers
- 2½ oz (75 g) bean threads
- 2T vegetable oil
- 3½ oz (100 g) ground meat
- 3T chopped onion
- 1¾ oz (50 g) cooked bamboo shoots, minced*
- 1t minced ginger root
- 2t curry powder
- 1T ketchup
- 1t soy sauce
- 1t salt
- 1t cornstarch
- Oil for deep-frying

*Available at the Oriental store.

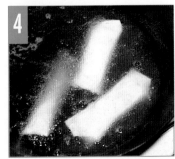

1. Soak bean threads in water to soften. Cut with scissor into small pieces. Drain water well.
2. In Chinese wok, heat 2T oil over medium-high heat; add chopped onion, bamboo shoots and ginger root. Stir fry for a few minutes; add curry powder and well drained bean threads. Toss and stir fry over medium heat.
3. Add ketchup, soy sauce, salt and mix well. Sprinkle cornstarch; mix well. Let it sit to cool or keep in a refrigirator.
4. Place wrapper in front of you and place about 1 heaping T of filling on top.
5. Fold sides in to overlap. Fold sides in to overlap again. Place a small amount of water or flour and water mixture at top of wrapper to seal.
6. Heat oil in wok to 350°F (180°C). Deep-fry rolls for 2 to 3 minutes or golden brown. Drain and let stand for a few minutes. Cut in half if you desire.

For those who are calorie conscious:
Place spring rolls on lightly greased baking sheet and bake for 4 to 5 minutes, turn once and bake for another 4 to 5 minutes.

TOFU TEMPURA

It is simple to make, yet very nutritious and tasty.

Deep-frying
....

2 servings INGREDIENTS

1 block firm *tofu*, well drained
Some cornstarch or all-purpose flour

Oil for deep-frying

***Tempura* Sauce:**
1/2 C *dashi* stock or chicken broth
1/4 C light color soy sauce
1T *mirin*, Japanese sweet cooking wine
1t cornstarch plus 1t water

Garnishes:
Chopped scallion
Grated fresh ginger root
Bonito flakes

1. Drain *tofu* well. Place *tofu* on a cutting boad and tilt to one side, or place *tofu* between two sheets of paper towels to drain.
2. Cut *tofu* into fourths. Coat *tofu* with cornstarch or all-purpose flour.
3. Heat deep-frying oil to 350°F (175°C). Deep fry *tofu* until lightly browned. Drain.
4. Mix all *tempura* sauce ingredients in a small sauce pan; heat until sauce thickens.
5. Place fried *tofu* in an individual bowl and pour sauce over.
6. Sprinkle with scallion, ginger root and bonito flakes.

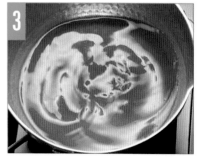

These rice balls are ideal for picnics.

Rice

3 C cooked rice, still warm rice

Filling A:
2 large pickled plums, seeds removed

Filling B:
3 T dried bonito flakes
1 t soy sauce
Mix bonito flakes and soy sauce

1. Have a bowl of cold water near by you so that your hands can be dampen to prevent rice from sticking to them.
2. In the palm of your hand, place about 1 C of rice and form it into a ball with cupped hands.
3. Make an indentation in the center and fill it with A or B. Work the rice into a ball again.
4. Press down with your hand to flatten the ball then shape into triangle. Wrap with seaweed.

GRILLED RICE BALLS

The aroma of mild soy sauce stimulates the appetite.

Rice

3 C cooked rice, still warm rice*

2 T soy sauce

Filling A:
2 large pickled plums
Remove seeds

Filling B:
3 T dried bonito flakes
1 t soy sauce
Mix flakes and soy sauce
*See page 90 for cooking rice.

1. Have a bowl of cold water near by you so that your hands can be dampened to prevent rice from sticking to them.
2. In the palm of your hand, place about 1 C of rice and form it into a ball with cupped hands.
3. Make an indentation in the center and fill it with A or B.
4. Work the rice into a ball again.
5. Press down with your hand to flatten the ball, then shape into a triangle.
6. Baste with soy sauce on both sides. Grill until outside is crispy.

LEMON RICE BALLS

Toasted seaweed and lemon zest provide A distinctive flavor to these rice balls.

Rice

 INGREDIENTS

2 stuffed rice balls*　See page 81
1t　salt
1t　toasted sesame seeds
1/4t　grated lemon peel
1/2 sheet *nori* seaweed

Coat rice ball with salt, sesame seeds and lemon peel mixture and wrap with seaweed.

STUFFED SQUID WITH RICE

Rice

Rice filling makes this dish special. Cut into thick slices.

2 servings INGREDIENTS

1 whole squid
½C leftover rice
1t salt
1T peas, cooked

Simmering Broth:
1¼C *kombu* kelp stock
1t sugar
1T *mirin*, Japanese sweet
  cooking wine
1T light-color soy sauce

1. Hold the tail toward you. Push body up so that cuttlebone slips out.
2. Grasp tail with left hand, pull tentacles and entrails. Make slit at the base of tentacles. Do not break ink bag. Remove eyes and mouth. Remove entrails.
3. Rub with salt to remove sliminess. Pull the skin off. Wash under running water.
4. Put tentacles in boiling water and cook for 2 minutes. Blanch in cold water and drain. Cut into small pieces.
5. Mix rice and tentacles; add cooked peas and 1t salt.
6. Stuff rice mixture in a body case. Secure end with a bamboo skewer.
7. Put squid in a pot and cover with simmering broth; cook over medium heat with lid on for 20 minutes, turning once. Cut into serving sizes.

RICE PORRIDGE WITH GRILLED SALMON

A favorite on a cold day.

Rice

serving INGREDIENTS

½C cooked rice*
   See page 90 for cooked
   rice.
1 small piece salmon fillet
1t *sake*
Salt and pepper to taste
1C soup stock
½t light-color soy sauce

1. Cut salmon steak fillet into serving size pieces.
2. In a saucepan, heat soup stock and add salmon; cook until color changes. Add *sake* and cooked rice; cook on low heat for 15 minutes.

RICE PORRIDGE WITH TURTLE SOUP

Rice

This dish is easily digested and quite refreshing.

1 serving INGREDIENTS

$2/3$C cooked rice
1 can 6 oz (180g) turtle soup
$1/2$C of water
$1/2$T *sake*
$1/4$t salt
$1/4$t light-color soy sauce
1 egg
$1/2$T chopped green onion

TURTLE SOUP

Clear soup broth is made from turtle flesh.

1. In an earthen ware pot, mix turtle soup and water; add *sake*, salt and light-color soy sauce and bring to boiling.
2. Add cooked rice and cook over low hat until a boil is reached.
3. Add beaten egg over and cook until egg is settled. Sprinkle chopped green onion on top.

If you use leftover cold rice, rinse under running water to remove gluten for best result.

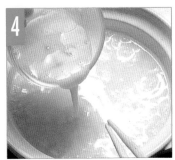

GARNISHED RICE WITH GREEN TEA

This is a very refreshing dish.

Rice

1 serving INGREDIENTS

²/₃ C cooked rice
 *See page 90 for cooked rice
1 large pickled plum (ume-boshi), stone removed
¹/₄ sheet of *nori* seaweed
¹/₂ T toasted sesame seeds
1 C hot green tea

1. Place cooked rice in a bowl; pour hot green tea on top.
2. Chop plum into two to three pieces; place on rice.
3. Cut *nori* seaweed into thin strips by scissor; sprinkle on rice.

CRISPY FRIED NOODLES

Noodles

This recipe reflects the Chinese influence with the use of fresh ginger root and *shiitake* mushrooms.

1 to 2 servings INGREDIENTS

1 package fresh made Chinese noodles
3½ oz (100 g) cabbage
⅔ oz (20 g) carrot
1 dry *shiitake*, Chinese mushroom
½ squid fillet
1 green pepper, cut into chunks
3 oz (80 g) chicken breast, deboned

Marinade Sauce:
¼t ginger juice
¼t soy sauce
¼t *sake* or cooking wine

½T cornstarch plus 1T water
½ cube chicken bouillon
½C *shiitake* soaking water
2t *sake*
½T soy sauce
¼t sugar
A pinch of salt
½ clove minced garlic
¼t sesame oil
Deep-frying oil for noodles

1. Heat deep-frying oil to 350°F (180°C). Deep-fry noodles. Set aside. Keep warm.
2. Chop cabbage. Cut carrot into half lengthwise and slice thin. Cook carrot until tender. Soak *shiitake* mushroom in water and reserve the water. Cut *shiitake* into quarter-rounds.
3. Lay squid fillet on cutting board, inner surface down. Score the outer surface with many shallow cuts in a cross-hatch design. Cut into serving sizes.
4. Cut chicken into small bite size pieces; marinate in marinade sauce for 10 minutes.
5. Dissolve chicken bouillon cube with *shiitake* soaking water. Mix cornstarch and water. Set aside.
6. Heat 1T oil in wok; stir-fry garlic to release aroma; add carrot, cabbage, mushroom, squid, green pepper and chicken pieces. Stir-fry for 2 to 3 minutes. Pour in chicken stock.
7. Add *sake*, soy sauce and salt. Stir-fry for 2 to 3 minutes. Add cornstarch mixture and stir until thickened. Sprinkle sesame oil. Serve over deep-fried noodles.

STIR-FRIED THICK NOODLES

This enchanting combination of noodles and vegetables can be served as a light lunch.

Noodles

1 to 2 servings INGREDIENTS

1 package fresh made noodles
1 slice pork loin (2 1/2 oz '75g))
1/2 onion
1 green onion
1 cabbage leaf
1/3 bean sprouts
1T curry powder

1T soy sauce
1T water

1/2T butter or margarine
1T vegetable oil

1. Melt butter in a skillet over medium heat. Stir-fry noodles until partially browned. Set aside and keep warm.
2. Cut pork into serving pieces. Cut onion into chuncks. Cut green onion 1 1/2 in. (4cm) in length. Chop up cabbage.
3. Heat 1T oil in skillet over medium heat; stir-fry pork until color turns whitish. Add onion, green onion and cabbage; stir-fry for 5 minutes or until all vegetables are tender.
Mix curry powder with water.
4. Add curry powder mixture and stir well. Add soy sauce and stir well. Serve over hot noodles.

INFORMATION

This section provides a working knowledge of the basic cutting and cooking techniques, and helpful tips necessary in the preparation of successful meals.

PREPARATION

Rice Cooking

There are two types of rice available; white short-grain rice and white long-grain rice. Use white short-grain rice for Japanese dishes. The short-grain rice is more glutinous than the long-grain rice. In the U.S., short-grain rice is grown extensively in California. Newly cropped rice needs less water and slightly shorter cooking time than old rice. A little practice is needed to make perfect rice, however if you cook a lot of rice, an automatic rice cooker will make your work a lot easier, so it's a good investment.

Rice increases in volume as it cooks, twice to three times, depending on the kind of rice you use. The following is a key to shiny and fluffy rice. Go ahead with these basic tips for successful rice cooking. It's easy.

1. Measure rice carefully.
2. Wash rice in a big bowl of water. Rub grains gently since wet grains break easily.
3. Remove any bran or polishing agent. Drain off water well. Repeat this step until water is almost clear.
4. To make fluffy and moist rice, set rice aside for at least 30 minutes in summer and one hour in winter. This allows ample time for rice to absorb water.
5. In cooking pot, add rice and correct amount of water. Cover with lid.
6. Cook rice over medium heat until water boils. Do not bring it to boiling point quickly. If the quantity of rice is large, cook rice over high heat from the beginning. The heat can be carried into the center of rice if cooked over medium heat.
7. When it begins to boil, turn heat to high and cook for 1 minute. Never lift lid while cooking.
8. Turn heat to low and cook for 4 to 5 minutes (Be careful not to overboil). Then the pot begins to steam.
9. Reduce heat to the lowest for 10 minutes.
10. Turn off the heat and let rice stand covered for 10 minutes. During these 10 minutes the grains are allowed to "settle", and the cooking process is completed by the heat retained in the rice and the walls of the pot.

TOFU PREPARATION TIPS

Fresh *tofu* is very fragile.
It is best to use fresh *tofu* within 24 hours after it is made. If it is not to be used right away, drain out water from the original container; add cold water and seal tight. Or place *tofu* in a flat-bottomed container and fill with water and cover. Keep *tofu* in the bottom of refrigerator. *Tofu* can be kept fresh for 3 to 4 days. If kept more than 3 to 4 days, it is recommended that *tofu* be boiled in salted water for 2 to 3 minutes. Do not freeze because the texture of *tofu* will change. However, if you prefer a different texture, you may try as follows: 1. Drain water from water-packed container. 2. Wrap *tofu* in plastic sheet. 3. Keep in freezer. 4. Color turns to light umber. This way frozen *tofu* can be stored indefinitely. Before cooking dip in water and remove plastic sheet and wash well. Frozen *tofu* has tender and meaty texture and makes excellent dishes with vegetables. To cook fresh *tofu*, do not overcook. Always add *tofu* last in cooking. Also for better cooking, drain water out before cooking. It gives a firmer and richer flavor. Keep *tofu* in refrigerator for a couple of hours or overnight. Or faster results, see illustration below. For faster results, place *tofu* on several layers of towels on cutting board and top with water-filled bowl. Change the towels often.

Cut *tofu* into cubes.

Cut *tofu* into ¼-inch (0.7 cm) or ½-inch (1.5 cm) thick slices.

Cut *tofu* crosswise into halves; then slice into 8 pieces.

PREPARATION

Basic Cutting Methods

When preparing ingredients, use a sharp knife. Cut to bite size pieces making them easy to cook and to eat.

For decorative cuts, use the tip of knife. For peeling, use the lower part of blade. The part from the center towards the tip is used for most cutting techniques.

Rounds

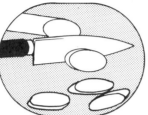

Round ingredients such as *daikon* radish or carrot are cut into the same thickness.

Diagonal Slices

Thin round ingredients such as cucumber are sliced diagonally giving an enlarging effect.

"Paring" Thin Fillets

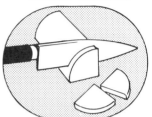

Soft or fragile ingredients are placed flat and pared off with the knife parallel to the cutting board.

Quarter Rounds

Large round ingredients such as turnip or *daikon* radish are split into quarters and then sliced.

Half-rounds

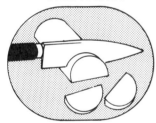

Large round ingredients such as *daikon* radish are split into halves and sliced.

Wedges

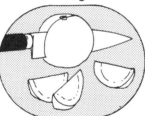

Ingredients such as lemon or onion are split into quarters then eighths.

Rolling Wedges

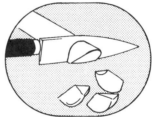

Ingredients are rolled and cut diagonally to give more sides for seasoning.

Rectangles

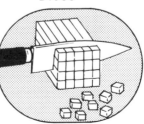

Large ingredients such as *daikon* radish are cut into 2 in (5cm) length and then sliced into $\frac{1}{2}$ in (1.5cm) thickness.

Shreds

Ingredients are sliced into thin rectangles of 2–2$\frac{1}{2}$ in (5–6.5cm) length, layered and cut into thin match-like sticks parallel to the fibers.

Sticks

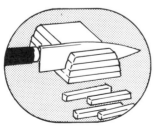

Ingredients such as potato, carrot or bamboo shoots are cut into 2–2$\frac{1}{2}$ in (5–6.5cm) long, $\frac{3}{8}$ in (1cm) wide sticks.

Dices

Ingredients are cut into $\frac{3}{8}$ in (1cm) wide sticks, and then into $\frac{3}{8}$ in (1cm) cubes.

Mincing

Shredded ingredients such as ginger root or green onion are chopped finely.

91

COOKING TIPS

Deep-frying

Tempura represents all "batter-fried" foods in Japan. It is probably the best known Japanese dish.

Four points for successful *Tempura*
1) Fresh ingredients.
2) Good vegetable oil.
3) Constant frying temperature.
4) Lumpy batter.

Prepare all ingredients to be deep-fried ahead of time. Preferably keep them in a refrigerator until the last minute. Make the *tempura* batter just before the actual deep-frying. The *tempura* batter, mixture of ice water, eggs and flour, should never be stirred well. Mix lightly — batter should be lumpy. All foods should be thoroughly dried before dredging. If you prefer a thick coating to thin batter, use less ice water than the recipe.

In general, deep-frying requires a large amount of oil in the wok, heavy cast iron skillet or deep-fryer. The use of polyunsaturated vegetable oil is strongly recommended for deep-frying. None of the pure vegetable oils contains cholesterol. The right temperature for deep-frying is 330°–355°F (165°–180°C). The oil should reach this temperature before any ingredients are added. An easy way to tell whether the oil has reached the desired temperature is adding a drop of batter into the oil. If the drop of batter reaches the bottom and slowly returns to the surface, the oil is not yet hot enough. If the batter drops half way to the bottom and immediately bounces up to the surface, the oil is ready for deep-frying. Drop in ingredients and deep-fry until golden. Adjust the temperature to maintain a constant frying temperature. Frying temperature of 340°F (170°C) is recommended for vegetables. Use deep-frying thermometer to maintain a constant oil temperature. Skim the surface of the oil occasionally to keep it clean. Start with vegetables and then shrimp which requires a higher temperature. The oil used for deep-frying can be saved and re-used. To grant your oil longer life, remove crumbs with a fine mesh strainer. The quality of used oil is judged by its clarity, not by the number of times used nor the length of time used. Fresh oil is light in color and clear. If the used oil is still relatively clear, it is readily usable again. For the second time round, it is recommended to deep-fry chicken or meats coated with bread crumbs. To remove odor in oil, deep-fry some potatoes uncoated. The moisture in potato absorbs odor while it is deep-fried. The proportion of 3:1 (used oil: fresh oil) is also usable again for deep-frying meats and chicken, but not for *tempura*. To store the used oil, first strain with a fine mesh strainer while oil is still hot. Then place the oil in a heatproof container and allow to cool. Cover and store in dark and cool place or in the refrigerator.

Grilling, Broiling, Pan-frying, Baking, Barbecueing

The grilling method is used to cook food quickly over very high heat so that the outside is crisp while the inside flesh remains tender and moist. The ingredients must be fresh. Grilling can be done with two different ways; direct and indirect heat. If you do charcoal grill, prepare charcoal fire in advance so that heat gets very hot. For stove top grilling, coat the rack with thin film of oil, then heat the unit before you place food on. Fish and meats are often marinated or basted with marinade sauces before and during cooking. Marinade sauces are combinations of *sake, mirin* or sugar, soy sauce and fresh ginger which has the same tenderizing enzyme as papaya and pineapple. Grill 60% on one side and 40% on the other side. For pan-frying, heat and add a small amount of oil. Heat the oil, then tilt the skillet so the oil covers the surface. When the oil begins to form a light haze, it is ready to pan-fry the ingredients. Cook over high heat, so that fish or meat except pork is tender and moist inside and the flavor is sealed in. If longer cooking is necessary, reduce heat and cover for a few minutes. You may need to add some marinade sauce to the pan. Then remove the lid and continue to cook until all liquid evaporates. For oven baking, preheat the oven to the required temperature and place food in the center of the oven to allow for even baking.

Nabemono Cooking (one-pot dishes)

Nabemono includes any dish that is cooked in one pot and eaten on the table. Therefore it has a great many varieties besides *sukiyaki* and *shabu-shabu,* and one of the main characteristics is in the cooking stock. In *sukiyaki* you only pick up solid ingredients from the pot, while in fish stew you take the broth together and enjoy it as a soup. In *shabu-shabu* or *mizutaki* or chicken hot pot you take the cooked but unseasoned ingredients and dip into sauces. In *oden-nabe* fish products and vegetables are stewed for a long time and eaten with the broth. In any type of *nabemono,* you can choose any ingredients you like. Basically *nabemono* needs no special cooking technique, but there are several points: When selecting ingredients, think not only of the colors but the affinity. Avoid harsh-tasting or strong-odor or fragile food. When preparing, cut each ingredient according to its cooking time so that all ingredients are ready to eat at the same time. Some foods need parboiling. *Daikon* radish and *konnyaku* must be parboiled to remove harsh taste. Dried foods should be softened well.

Simmering

Simmering food requires a special preparation for the cooking broth:
1) Simmering liquid is generally made of seasoned stock.
2) You may need some special cutting techniques for vegetables such as diagonal slices, flower-cuts, trimming to enhance the appearance of the finished dish.
3) Some ingredients need parboiling to remove harsh or bitter taste and rawness. Also, some ingredients take longer to cook. These ingredients are sometimes pre-cooked in different pans, then added to the simmering liquid.
   Simmered food can be served as a single dish or as one-pot dish. The ingredients and simmering liquid for the one-pot dishes are prepared ahead of time and arranged attractively on large platters.
The size of the pot is determined by the amount of ingredients to be cooked. A thick-bottomed pot will distribute the heat more evenly. If simmering for longer time, use a deep pot that holds an ample amount of simmering liquid. Slow electric cooker will have the same effect.
Use light seasoning for simmering liquid. The less the better. You can always add more later. In general add sugar or *mirin* first, then salt, rice vinegar (if recipe calls for) and soy sauce. Remember to control simmering temperature so that the liquid can be slowly absorbed into the ingredients.

COOKING TIPS

Steaming

Steaming is one of the best way of retaining more nutrients and natural flavor than other conventional means of cooking. Steaming seals in the natural juices of meats and vegetables which are delicious when served over rice.

There are many different types of steamers. Wok with a cover will work as a good steamer. Multitiered bamboo steamers may be purchased. However, a large pot with a cover will suffice for the purpose of steaming food.

Steaming racks are necessary to support and elevate the plate or bowl which holds food steamed in a wok. A round cake rack will do just as well as commercially available steaming racks. You may improvise water chestnut cans with both ends removed. The rack should be put in the center of the wok or pan.

All steamers operate according to the same basic principle. The efficient circulation of steam is of paramount importance. Bamboo steamers have several tiers in which many dishes can be steamed simultaneously. The tiers and cover are set on top of a wok containing boiling water. There are also metal steamers consisting of a pot to hold the water, usually two tiers and a cover. For example, the bottom pot cooks soup stock while the two tiers are used to steam two other separate dishes. In this manner, many dishes may be steamed at once saving time and energy. Follow the steps below for effective steaming:

1) Pour water into the wok or pot so that the water level stands one inch below the steaming rack or dish of food.
2) Cover the wok and bring the water to a full boil.
3) Use only heatproof dishes for steaming.
4) Place the dish of food atop the steaming rack. Cover and bring to the boiling point again. Turn the temperature down to medium high and allow to steam for the specified time.
5) Check the water level when longer steaming is necessary.

Stir-frying, Sautéing

This cooking method combines the elements of high heat and constant tossing to seal in the flavor and juices of meat and vegetables. Thus, this technique is often used for Chinese cooking. Stir-frying cooks protein foods thoroughly at the same time leaving them tender and juicy. Vegetables retain their natural color and crisp texture when stir-fried. It is important that slices are uniform in size so that they can be cooked evenly. Some vegetables may need parboiling before stir-frying. Prepare all necessary seasonings before stir-frying. Heat the wok or skillet until it barely gets hot and add a small amount of oil (usually 2 T), then roll the oil around to cover the surface of the wok. When the oil begins to form a light haze, add the ingredients. Follow the recipe and remember to adjust the temperature control at the proper stir-frying temperature. Actual stir-frying involves vigorous arm action in the constant stirring and tossing of the food. Serve immediately while still hot.

UTENSILS

LACQUER WARE

For serving foods lacquer ware is widely used in Japanese tables. New ones have some odor, so wipe them with vinegar, using lint free soft cloth. Leave it in well ventilated dark place. Do not use dish soap. Avoid prolonged soaking in hot or cold water. To retain beautiful glossy shine, dab on a bit of oil with cotton and wipe off thoroughly with a soft cloth. Be careful not to scratch them with finger nails or ring. To store wrap with tissue paper. Do not put in the dishwasher.

MEASURING UTENSILS

Measuring by the eye often causes waste of food or failure of seasoning. Be sure to measure in the right way.

[Kitchen Scales]
For home use, choose 5 lb/2 kg scales, with a large dish. Flat plate does not hold flour or nuts well. Do not leave things on the dish as it damages the spring.

[Measuring Cup]
1 cup is equivalent to 240 ml in this book. Usually made of glass, stainless or plastic. Stainless cups are most durable while glass ones are easy to read.

[Measuring Spoons]
There are four graduated sizes, tablespoon (T), teaspoon (t), half teaspoon ($\frac{1}{2}$ t), and quarter teaspoon ($\frac{1}{4}$ t). 1 tablespoon is equivalent to 15 ml or 3 teaspoons. 1 teaspoon equals 5 ml. To measure dry ingredients, scoop into appropriate spoon until full, and level with a spatula/knife.

METAL STRAINER

Ideal for straining dry and liquid ingredients and also useful for sifting small amount of dry ingredients.

MICROWAVE RANGE

For cooking foods speedily and cleanly. Without heating the utensils or oven, only the foods are heated. The food must contain moisture, and metal container or china with metal decorations are not suitable (metals cause sparks). Microwaves do a good job in thawing frozen meats or fish.

OVEN THERMOMETER

Success of baking lies in the accurate oven temperature, so it is a good investment.

NON-STICK MUFFIN PAN and COOKIE SHEET

It is made of rustproof alminum. Before using for the first time and after each use, wash in hot suds and dry. Pre-condition by rubbing in small amount of salad oil on surface.

ONION CHOPPER

This tool is useful for chopping onion or nuts into small pieces without a risk to fingers.

UTENSILS

OVEN WARE

This baking dish is safe for oven and microwave use. It can go from freezer to oven and is dishwasher-safe.

ROLLING PIN

This is useful tool to make pastries or pasta. Some recipe calls for rolling the dough as thin as possible with floured stockinet-covered rolling pin.

PRESSURE COOKER

Cooking by superheated steam under pressure reduces cooking time to $1/4$–$1/5$ of what conventional pan takes.

VEGETABLE STEAMER

For steaming food successfully, advance preparation of steamer is just as important as assembling ingredients. The steamer is adjustable according to the amount of food and size of pot you use.

WOK

There are round-bottomed and flat-bottomed, or one-handled and two-handled types. For home use, round bottomed ones with side handles are recommended. Materials should be cast-iron since stainless scorches easily and Teflon-coats are easily scarred. Cast-iron woks are multi-purpose pots; stir-frying, deep-frying, simmering and steaming with bamboo steamer.

BAMBOO SKEWERS

For Japanese cooking, bamboo skewers are a very handy tool. They are not only used for many grilled dishes, but to test foods for doneness by pricking and also for cooking raw shrimp; to prevent curling while boiling. They come in various sizes.

Moisten bamboo skewers before skewering for grilling to prevent breaking or burning. Wash and store them or throw away after one or several uses. Bamboo is a versatile plant; for centuries it's been proven in the Orient. You can use bamboo for various things: houses, furniture, fences, cooking utensils and so on. Bamboo shoots are edible while bamboo leaf is used as a wrapper.

GARLIC PRESS

Used to crush garlic cloves.

INGREDIENTS

ANISE STAR —— Brown, star-shaped seed with the taste of licorice. Keeps indefinitely.

ATSUAGE (deep-fried *tofu* cutlet) • ABURA-AGE (deep-fried *tofu* pouch) ——
Atsuage is a deep-fried regular *tofu*. It is fried until the outside becomes crisp and golden brown but the inside is still white. *Abura-age* is also deep-fried *tofu*, but before frying it is cut into thin sheets.

BAMBOO SHOOTS —— Bamboo shoots are one of the most common ingredients in Asian cooking. In Japan, bamboo shoot are "cooked-fresh" canned in water and available all the year round. Occasionally, such water-packed bamboo shoots is exported and available in U.S..

BEAN THREADS —— These are long, dry noodles made of mung bean flour. They keep on the shelf indefinitely. Soak them in warm water for 15 minutes before use. They may also be deep fried in hot oil. Do not soak them in water prior to deep-frying though. Use them as a noodle in soups, or with stir-fried vegetables and meat. To keep them as clean as possible place them in a large paper bag before removing wrapper. Break off the amount needed and store remainder in a bag.

BURDOCK ROOT (*gobou*) —— Fresh burdock root has reddish-brown color; about 1–1$\frac{1}{2}$ feet long with brown earth still clinging to them. Wash and scarpe or peel as you need it.

CHINESE CABBAGE (bok choy) —— This versatile, greenish-white leafed cabbage is used in stir-fry and one-pot dishes. It is also added to soups, and made into pickles. A heavy, succulent vegetable, Chinese caggage is often found in supermarkets, not to mention in Oriental food stores. It is also known as "celery cabbage" and "*nappa* (sometimes '*Napa*') cabbage". Avoid produce with spotted leaves, if possible. Store the same as you would lettuce.

CHINESE MUSTARD, DRIED —— Pungent powder. Mix 1 tablespoon dry powder with 1 tablespoon water for average proportion. Store dry powder on shelf indefinitely.

DAIKON RADISH —— *Daikon* radish is rich in vitamins, and its leaves contain much calcium. This radish is thought to aid digestion of oily foods. It is good for simmered dishes.

DRIED BONITO —— This is an important ingredient in *dashi* stock. A stick of dried bonito looks like a 6–8 in. (15–20 cm) long brownish hunk of wood.
Shaved, dried bonito flakes are also available in packs and convenient to use.
Dried bonito "thread" shavings are often used as a garnish. Such "thread" shavings look like rosy-beige excelsior and have a pleasant flavor. If you cannot obtain them, use regular dried bonito flakes.

EGGPLANTS —— Japanese eggplants that are on the average 4 in. (10 cm) long and weigh 2–3 oz (60–90 g) each. Because size varies with region and season, weights are included to offer a guideline.

INGREDIENTS

ENOKI MUSHROOMS —— *Enoki* mushrooms are mild-flavored and have a pleasant crispness aroma. They are often used in soups. There are canned *enoki* mushrooms but fresh ones are better.

GANMODOKI (deep-fried *tofu* burger) —— *Ganmodoki* consists of crumbled *tofu*, sesame seeds, ginkgo nuts and slivered vegetables like carrots, mushrooms, and burdock bound together with grated mountain yam. This *tofu*-based mixture is formed into 3 in. (8 cm) patties or 1½ in. (4 cm) balls, then deep-fried. They are used in simmered dishes. They go well with soy sauce.

GINGER ROOT —— Ginger is a pungent, aromatic root stalk of a genus Zingiber, tropical Asiatic and Polinesian herb. It is a popular spice all over the world.
The pungent substance promotes both appetite and digestion.
When using for stir-fried dishes, shred and cook in hot oil to extract the aroma. In this oil cook the other ingredients. Choose fresh root without wrinkles.

GRILLED *TOFU* (yaki-dofu) —— Grilled *tofu* is grilled on both sides over charcoal, thus producing its firm texture. It is easy to recognize by the light mottling on the skin. If *yaki-dofu* is not available, you can make it easily. Drain regular *tofu* and lightly grill each side of *tofu* over high heat. Grilled *tofu* is often used in boiled dishes such as *sukiyaki*.

HANPEN (fish meat product) —— HANPEN is made mainly from fish protein. Good *Hanpen* is white and soft and spongy texture. Keep in a refrigerator.

HIJIKI (black sea vegetable) —— Dried *Hijiki* is black and brittle vegetable. Soaking makes *hijiki* tender and lustrous vegetable rich in calcium.

HOISIN SAUCE —— Pungent, sweet condiment sauce made of soy beans, spices, chili and sugar. Once opened, store in a jar with tight lid. Keeps refrigerated for about 6 months.

HOT BEAN PASTE (chili paste with beans) —— Broad bean sauce made from broad beans, chili peppers and sometimes garlic. Comes in cans or jars. Refrigerated, keeps indifinitely in tightly sealed jars. Degree of hotness may vary between different brands.

IKURA (salmon roe) —— Salmon roe mildly seasoned with salt, often in bright color. It is eaten like caviar.

JAPANESE CUCUMBER —— Recipes in this book call for Japanese cucumbers, which are equivalent to ½ or ⅓ American cucumbers. If using American type, peel and seed cucumbers unless skin is delicate and thin and seeds are immature. If using the Japanese variety, it is not necessary to peel or seed. However to smooth the rough surface and to bring out the skin color, dredge the cucumber in salt and roll it back and forth on a cutting board using the palm of your hand. Wash well.

INGREDIENTS

JAPANESE HOT PEPPER ——— Red pepper is used fresh or dried. Dried and ground coarse pepper is called *ichimi*, or one-flavor spice. This *ichimi* is one of the ocmponent ingredients of *shichimi* or 7-spice mixture. *Shichimi* is a collection of seven dried and ground flavors: red pepper flakes (*togarashi*); roughly ground, brown *sansho* pepper pods; minute flakes of dried mandarin orange peel; dark green *nori* seaweed bits; black kemp seeds; white poppy seeds; and black sesame seeds.

KAMABOKO·CHIKUWA (steamed fish paste) ——— *Kamaboko* is made mainly from fish protein. Good *kamaboko* is white and elastic and the cut end is glossy. Keep in refrigerator. *Chikuwa* literally means ring of bamboo. Both *kamaboko* and *chikuwa* go well with horseradish soy sauce.

KOCHU JANG (hot sauce) ——— This hot sauce is used for Korean cooking. The sauce is made from glutenous rice powder, chili powder and some other malts.

KOMBU (kelp) ——— *Kombu* is one of the basic ingredients used for making *dashi* stock. When you use it, never wash or rinse. The speckled surface of the kelp holds flavor. Kelp contains the most iodine of all seaweeds.

KONNYAKU·ITO-KONNYAKU ——— *Konnyaku* made from the roots of "devil's tongue" has no calories. It must be parboiled before eating. *Ito-konnyaku* are knonnyaku strips.

MENTAIKO (cod fish roe) ——— Bright red color comes from food color and red chili powder and the chili powder is added to *MENTAIKO* (cod fish roe).

MOUNTAIN YAMS (glutinous yams) ——— A fuzzy beige glutinous yams are eaten raw after being peeled. After being grated this tuber root gets thick snowy white and sticky. Can stay fresh for a week.

MOZUKU (a kind of sea vegetation) ——— This is a mass of brownish black sea vegetable with slightly slippery texture. *MOZUKU* is an excellent source of minerals and calcium.

MIRIN ——— *Mirin* is heavily sweetened *sake*, used for cooking. *Mirin* is called "sweet cooking rice wine". *Sake* sweetened with sugar can be substituted.

MISO ——— *Miso* is fermented soybean paste. The colors range from yellow to brown; yellow *miso* is referred to as white *miso* in this book. Brown *miso* is called red *miso*. Since there are various kinds of *miso*, it might be helpful to learn about *miso* by buying small quantities of various kinds. It is used for soups, dressings, sauces, etc..

NAMEKO MUSHROOMS ——— Canned or water-packed *NAMEKO* mushrooms have slippery, almost slimy substance and have golden brownish color. They have a rich earthy flavor. Use within 3-4days once you opened.

INGREDIENTS

NATTO (fermented soy beans) —— This is fermented soy beans preparation made by the action of special bacteria. It has a rich cheese-like aroma and flavor and is sticky. With good *natto*, the sticky "threads" formed while mixing should be strong and stubborn and the beans should be moderately moist.

NORI SEAWEED —— The best quality *nori* seaweed is glossy black-purple. It is used after toasting which improves flavor and texture. *Nori* seaweed grows around bamboo stakes placed underwater. When the time comes, it is gathered, washed, laid in thin sheets and dried. It contains lots of protein.

OKURA (fuzzy green vegetable) —— Small green chili-shaped vegetable with fuzzy surface.

OYSTER SAUCE —— Thick brown sauce made from oysters and soy sauce. Used to enhance flavor as a dip. Keeps indefinitely in the refrigerator.

PANKO (dehydrated bread crumbs) —— Japanese dehydrated bread crumbs with a coarser texture. Regular bread crumbs are available at most supermarkets or Oriental groceries.

SAKE —— *Sake* is made by binoculating steamed mold (*koji*) and then allowing fermentation to occur. It is then refined. In Japan *sake* is the most popular beverage but it is also used in various ways in cooking.

SANSHO, KINOME SPRIGS —— Both the leaves and seed pods of *sansho* are used. Dried leaves are powdered and used as a spice, *sansho* pepper. The young leaves called *kinome* sprigs are mainly use garnish foods.

SESAME OIL —— Made from sesame seeds which are rich in oil and protein. This oil has a unique and aroma. It is mixed with salad oil and used for frying *tempura* or used to add flavor and aroma to the dressing used on Japanese-style *aemono* dishes.

SESAME SEEDS —— Both black and white sesame seeds are used in Japanese cooking. When toasted, sesame seeds have a much richer flavor. Still richer, however, are ground sesame seeds. To grind sesame seeds use a *suribachi* (Japanese grinding bowl). Before grinding, toast seeds in a dry frying pan. It is a nice garnish.

7-spice powder (*SHICHIMI-TOGARASHI*) —— This is a good spice for sprinkling over *udon*, *mizutaki*, etc. Because it loses its aroma quickly, buy it in small quantities and store, tightly covered.

SHIITAKE MUSHROOMS —— Both fresh and dried *shiitake* mushrooms can be obtained. Dried ones should be soaked in water before using. This soaking water makes *dashi* stock (Japanese soup stock). Fresh *shiitake* mushrooms have a distinctive, appealing "woody-fruity" flavor. *Shiitake* mushrooms are good for simmered dishes because of their special flavor. The best one has thick, brown velvety cap and firm fresh.

INGREDIENTS

SHIRASU (small and young sardine) —— Lightly seasoned with salt and dried petit fish.

SHISO LEAVES —— These minty, aromatic leaves come in green and red varieties. The red type to make *umeboshi* (pickled plum).

SHIMEJI MUSHROOMS —— Fresh *shimeji* mushrooms should be delicately crisp. The stems should be short and plump, and the flesh should be white. White mushrooms will do as substitute if *shimeji* mushrooms are not available.

SHISHAMO —— Small herring-like fish is sun dried and can be eaten whole fish with bones after lightly grilled.

SOY BEANS —— Soy beans were one of the "five sacred grains" of ancient China. They have cultivars including black and yellow ones and countless uses: they can be used in stews, turned it paste, soymilk, also *tofu*, and can be used as a meat substitute.

SOY SAUCE —— Soy sauce is made from soy beans and salt. It is the primary seasoning of Japanese cooking. It is used for simmered foods, dressings, soups; many kinds of Japanese dishes. Ordinary soy sauce is dark, but one which has a light color is also available. The light soy sauce does not darken the colors of food, and it is salty enough. Thick soy sauce is a good seasoning for raw fish, *sashimi*. It is rather sweet.

SNOW PEAS (Chinese pea pods) —— Flat edible pea pod. Has a delicate taste and comes fresh or frozen.

TOFU —— *Tofu*, "bean curd" in English, is an important product of soy beans. It is rich in protein, vitamins, calcium, and minerals. It is low in calories and saturated fats, and entirely free of cholesterol. There are two kinds of *tofu*; firm *tofu* and soft *tofu*.

TARAKO (cod fish roe) —— Prepared *TARAKO* has pink color.

TONKATSU SAUCE (dark, thick sauce) —— Japanese prepared sauce used as a dip for a pork cutlet.

TREFOIL (*mitsuba*) —— Trefoil is a member of the parsley family. The flavor is somewhere between sorrel and celery. It accents the flavor of many Japanese dishes.

UMEBOSHI —— *Umeboshi* are made every June when green plums come onto the market in Japan. Green, unripe plums are soaked in brine, packed with red shiso leaves and left to mature in the salty bath. In Japan *umeboshi* have long been regarded as a tonic. Not only are they thought to help in digestion they also keep the intestinal tract clean. This may be one of the reasons why *umeboshi* are served with the traditional Japanese breakfast. Also *umeboshi* paste can be a seasoning.

VINEGAR —— Japanese rice vinegar is milder than most Western vinegars. Lightness and relative sweetness are characteristics of rice vinegar. Use cider vinegar if substituting.

INGREDIENTS

VINEGARED FRESH GINGER
5–6 stalks young fresh ginger
Vinegar Mixture: $1/2$ C rice vinegar   2 T sugar   1 t salt $1/2$ C water
Bring vinegar mixture to a boil. Cool. Pour mixture into a glass. Cut leaves of fresh ginger, leaving about 9 in (23cm) of stem. Clean roots. Dip only the roots into boiling salted water. Remove immediately. Shake off water. Dip in vinegar mixture while hot.

WASABI —— *Wasabi* is Japanese horseradish. It is pale green in color. It has a more delicate aroma and is milder tasting than Western horseradish. In Japan both fresh and powdered *wasabi* are available, but it is hard to obtain fresh *wasabi* in other countries. The edible part of *wasabi* is the root. Usually it comes in a powdered form or in a tube, but the fragrance of fresh *wasabi* is much richer than powdered *wasabi*. The powder should be mixed with water to make a thick paste. *Wasabi* accompanies most fresh fish dishes, and also *Sushi*. Fresh fish may be hard to try for the first time, but with the added taste of soy sauce and *wasabi*, it will become one of your favorites.

YUZU CITRON —— Japanese citron. The fragrant rind is grated and added as a garnish to soups and other dishes. This citrus fruit appears also in Chinese and Korean cooking. In the West where *yuzu* citron is not often available, lemon or lime rind or zest can be used though neither is quite the same.

YAM NOODLE (*shirataki*) —— Thin transparent gelatin-like noodles, similar to bean threads. It is made from devil's tongue root, has no calories. *Konnyaku* (see page 99) made from the same root.

How To Soften Dried Foods

Dried *shiitake* mushrooms
Dried mushrooms must be soaked in warm water until soft, which takes about 1 hour. Place a flat pan lid, drop-lid, or any similar object on mushrooms to keep them submerged. Filling a bowl to the brim with water, adding mushrooms, or laying a plate (that has enough area to keep submerged) on top works just as well. Mushrooms soften quicker in warm water than in cold, and a drop-lid not only keeps mushrooms immersed but also prevents water from cooling off, which would slow the softening process. Discard stems and use only caps. Soaking liquid makes a good stock.

Dried bean threads
Another kind of gelatin noodle. This kind is easier to handls because it does not lose shape when cooked. To soften, soak in warm water until the center becomes transparent; drain.

Dried cloud ears (*kikurage*)
Black mushrooms which grow on mulberry trees. Look for well-dried whole mushrooms. Soak in water for 10 to 20 minutes until widely spread. Use luke warm water when in a hurry. Wash carefully and remove roots. They swell about 5 times after softening.

Dried *wakame* seaweed
Dried *wakame* seaweed increases its volume to 3–4 times when reconstituted. Cover with abundant water until the 'flesh' becomes thicker and flexible. Over-soaking will damage the texture. To draw out a fresh green color, blanch in boiling water and rinse in cold water at once. This method will also remove the odor.

METRIC TABLES

Today many areas of the world use the metric system and more will follow in the future. The following conversion tables are intended as a guide to help you.

General points of information that may prove valuable or of interest:
1 British fluid ounce = 28.5 ml
1 American fluid ounce = 29.5 ml

1 Japanese cup = 200 ml
1 British cup = 200 ml = 7 British fl oz
1 American cup = 240 ml = 8 American fl oz

1 British pint = 570 ml = 20 British fl oz
1 American pint = 470 ml = 16 American fl oz
T = tablespoon   oz = ounce   g = gram   ml = milliliter

Weights

ounces to grams*	grams to ounces
¼ oz = 7 g	1 g = 0.035 oz
½ oz = 14 g	5 g = ⅙ oz
1 oz = 30 g	10 g = ⅓ oz
2 oz = 60 g	28 g ≒ 1 oz
4 oz = 115 g	100 g = 3½ oz
6 oz = 170 g	200 g = 7 oz
8 oz = 225 g	500 g = 18 oz
16 oz = 450 g	1000 g = 35 oz

grams × 0.035 = ounces
ounces × 28.35 = grams

* Equivalent

Linear Measures

inches to centimeters	centimeters to inches*
½ in = 1.27 cm	1 cm = ⅜ in
1 in = 2.54 cm	2 cm = ¾ in
2 in = 5.08 cm	3 cm = 1⅛ in
4 in = 10.16 cm	4 cm = 1½ in
5 in = 12.7 cm	5 cm = 2 in
10 in = 25.4 cm	10 cm = 4 in
15 in = 38.1 cm	15 cm = 5¾ in
20 in = 50.8 cm	20 cm = 8 in

inches × 2.54 = centimeters
centimeters × 0.39 = inches

in = inch   cm = centimeter

Temperature

Fahrenheit (F) to Celsius (C)		Celsius (C) to Fahrenheit (F)	
freezer storage	−10°F = −23.3°C	freezer storage	−20°C = −4°F
	0°F = −17.7°C		−10°C = 14°F
water freezes	32°F = 0 °C	water freezes	0°C = 32°F
	68°F = 20 °C		10°C = 50°F
	100°F = 37.7°C		50°C = 122°F
water boils	212°F = 100 °C	water boils	100°C = 212°F
	300°F = 148.8°C		150°C = 302°F
	400°F = 204.4°C		200°C = 392°F

The water boiling temperature given is at sea level.

Conversion factors:

$$C = \frac{(F - 32) \times 5}{9}$$

$$F = \frac{C \times 9}{5} + 32$$

C = Celsius   F = Fahrenheit

INDEX